ESTATE PUBLICATIONS

BERKSHIRE

G000039446

Street maps with index
Administrative Districts
Population Gazetteer
Road Map with index
Postcodes

COUNTY RED BOOKS

This atlas is intended for those requiring street maps of the historical and commercial centres of towns within the county. Each locality is normally presented on one or two pages and although, with many small towns, this space is sufficient to portray the whole urban area, the maps of large towns and cities are for centres only and are not intended to be comprehensive. Such coverage in Super and Local Red Books (see page 2).

Every effort has been made to verify the accuracy of information in this book but the publishers cannot accept responsibility for expense or loss caused by any error or omission. Information that will be of assistance to the user of these maps will be welcomed.

The representation of a road, track or footpath on the maps in this atlas is no evidence of the existence of a right of way.

Street plans prepared and published by ESTATE PUBLICATIONS, Bridewell House, TENTERDEN, KENT. The Publishers acknowledge the co-operation of the local authorities of towns represented in this atlas.

Ordnance Survey® This product includes mapping data licensed from Ordnance Survey® with the permission of the Controller of Her Majesty's Stationery Office.

CONTENTS

COUNTY ADMINISTRATIVE DISTRICTS: pages 4-5

GAZETTEER INDEX TO ROAD MAP: pages 6-7
(with populations)

COUNTY ROAD MAP: pages 8-9

TOWN CENTRE STREET MAPS:

Arborfield	page 10	Old Windsor	45
Arborfield Cross	10	Pangbourne	30
Arborfield Garrison	10	Purley	31
Ascot	12	Reading	32-33
Bracknell	14-16	Sandhurst	34-35
Bray	17	Shinfield	42
Burghfield Common	17	Slough	36-37
Cookham	19	Sunningdale	13
Cookham Dean	18	Sunninghill	12
Cookham Rise	19	Thatcham	38-39
Crowthorne	20-21	Tilehurst	31
Datchet	22	Twyford	40
Eton	47	Uxbridge (Gtr London)	41
Finchampstead	43	Wargrave	42
Hungerford	23	Whitchurch	30
Lambourn	22	Wick Hill	43
Maidenhead	24-25	Windsor	46
Newbury	26-29	Winnersh	44
North Ascot	11	Wokingham	48-49

INDEX TO STREETS: pages 50-64

LEGEND TO STREET MAPS

One-Way Street	→	**Post Office**	●
Pedestrianized	▨	**Public Convenience**	⊙
Car Park	🅿	**Place of Worship**	+

Scale of street plans: 4 Inches to 1 mile (unless otherwise stated on the map).

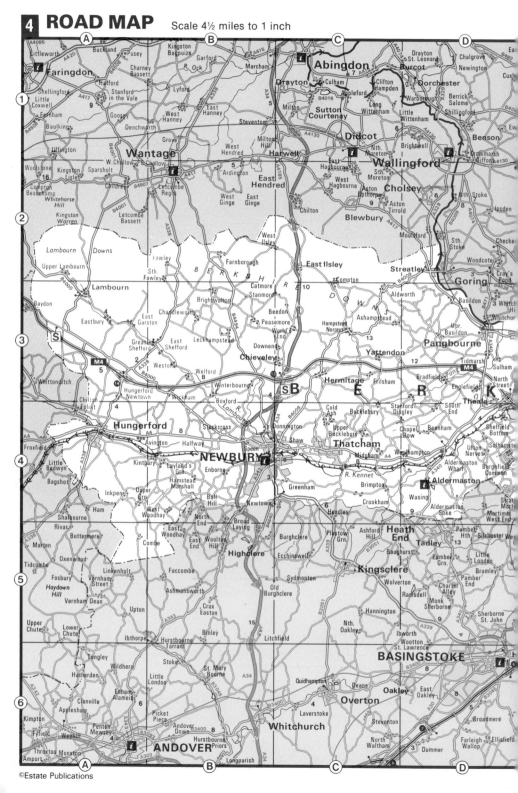

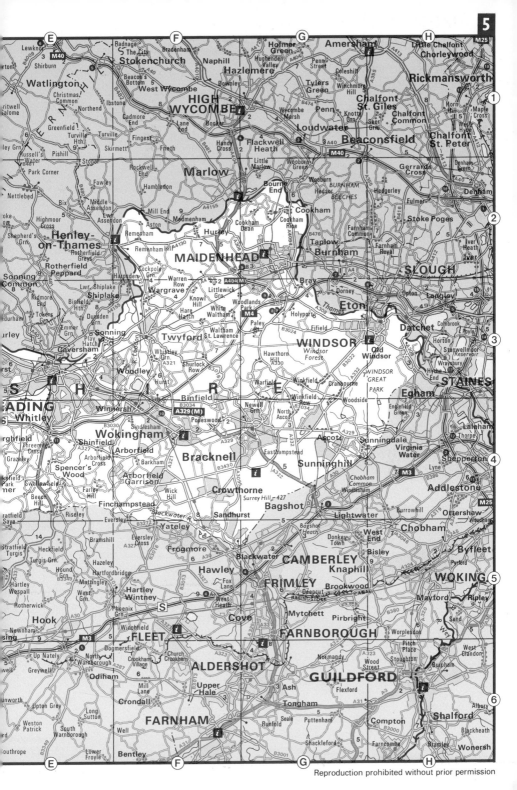

GAZETTEER INDEX TO ROAD MAP
with populations
County of Berkshire population 737,246

Districts:

Bracknell Forest	95,949
Newbury	136,700
Reading	128,877
Slough	101,066
Windsor & Maidenhead	132,465
Wokingham	139,189

Aldermaston 766	4 D4	Cookham Rise	5 G2
Aldermaston Soke	4 D4	Cox Green 7,616	*
Aldermaston Wharf	4 D4	Cranbourne	5 G3
Aldworth 248	4 C3	Crookham	4 C4
Arborfield &		Crowthorne 5,685	5 F4
Newland 2,252	5 F4	Datchet 4,947	5 H3
Arborfield Cross	5 E4	Donnington	
Arborfield Garrison	5 F4	(with Shaw) 1,573	4 C4
Ascot		Downend	4 C3
(Sunninghill) 11,025	5 G4	Earley 28,603	5 E4
Ashampstead 361	4 C3	East Garston 543	4 A3
Aston	5 F2	East Ilsley 434	4 C2
Avington	4 B4	East Shefford	4 B3
Barkham 2,957	5 F4	Eastbury	4 A3
Basildon 1,545	4 D3	Easthampstead	5 G4
Beech Hill 265	5 E4	Enborne 491	4 B4
Beedon 417	4 C3	Englefield 253	4 D3
Beenham 914	4 D4	Eton 3,656	5 G3
Binfield 5,238	5 F4	Farley Hill	5 E4
Bisham 1,126	5 F2	Farnborough 96	4 B2
Boxford 487	4 B4	Fawley 161	4 B2
Bracknell 50,325	5 F4	Finchampstead 11,772	5 F4
Bradfield 1,570	4 D3	Frilsham 317	4 C3
Bray 8,540	5 G3	Grazeley	5 E4
Brightwalton 285	4 B3	Great Shefford 912	4 B3
Brimpton 551	4 C4	Greenham 2,671	4 C4
Britwell 5,559	5 H2	Halfway	4 B4
Bucklebury 2,137	4 C4	Hampstead Norris 698	4 C3
Burghfield 5,740	5 E4	Hamstead Marshall 248	4 B4
Burghfield Common	4 D4	Hare Hatch	5 F3
Burghfield Hill	4 D4	Hawthorn Hill	5 G3
Calcot	4 D3	Hermitage 1,105	4 C3
Catmore 25	4 B3	Holyport	5 G3
Caversham	5 E3	Horton 942	5 H3
Chaddleworth 475	4 B3	Hungerford 5,183	4 A4
Chapel Row	4 D4	Hungerford Newtown	4 A4
Charvil 2,126	5 F3	Hurley 1,935	5 F2
Chieveley 2,517	4 C3	Hurst (St Nicholas) 1,692	5 F3
Cockpole Grn	5 F3	Inkpen 859	4 A4
Cold Ash 2,661	4 C4	Kintbury 2,472	4 B4
Combe 32	4 B5	Knowl Hill	5 F3
Compton 1,307	4 C3	Lambourn 3,740	4 A3
Cookham 5,752	5 G2	Langley	5 H3
Cookham Dean	5 G2	Leckhampstead 321	4 B3

Liitlewick Grn 5 F3
Maidenhead **50,159** 5 G2
Midgham **374** 4 C4
Mortimer 4 D4
Newbury **25,369** 4 B4
Newell Grn 5 G4
North Street 4 D3
Old Windsor **5,030** 5 H3
Padworth **545** *
Paley St 5 G3
Pangbourne **2,951** 4 D3
Peasemore **238** 4 B3
Popeswood 5 F4
Purley on Thames **4,141** 5 E3
Reading **114,822** 5 E4
Remenham **537** 5 F2
Riseley 5 E4
Ruscombe **1,026** 5 F3
Sandhurst **19,153** 5 F5
Shaw cum
 Donnington **1,573** 4 C4
Sheffield Bottom 4 D4
Shinfield **7,207** 5 E4
Shottesbrooke **132** *
Shurlock Row 5 F3
Sindlesham 5 F4
Slough **101,066** 5 H3
Sonning **1,354** 5 E3
South End 4 D4
South Fawley 4 B3
Speen **2,754** 4 B4
Spencer's Wood 5 E4
Stanford Dingley **222** 4 D4
Stanmore 4 C3
Stockcross 4 B4
Stratfield Mortimer **3,498** 4 D4
Streatley **986** 4 D2
Sulham **69** 4 D3
Sulhamstead **1,415** 4 D4
Sunningdale **4,489** 5 H4
Sunninghill **11,025** 5 G4
Swallowfield **1,677** 5 E4
Thatcham **20,226** 4 C4

Theale **9,998** 4 D4
Threemile Cross 5 E4
Tidmarsh **314** 4 D3
Tilehurst **14,055** 4 D3
Twyford **5,382** 5 F3
Ufton Nervet **343** 4 D4
Upper Basildon 4 D3
Upper Bucklebury 4 C4
Upper Green 4 B4
Upper Lambourn 4 A3
Upton 5 H3
Waltham St.
 Lawrence **1,232** 5 F3
Warfield **1,724** 5 G3
Wargrave **3,948** 5 F3
Warren Row 5 F3
Wasing **46** 4 D4
Welford **553** 4 B3
West Ilsley **334** 4 C2
West Woodhay **100** 4 B4
Weston 4 B3
Wexham Court **3,859** *
Whistley Green 5 F3
Whitchurch 4 D3
White Waltham **2,961** 5 F3
Whitley 5 E4
Wick Hill 5 F4
Wickham 4 B4
Windsor **32,444** 5 G3
Winkfield **13,824** 5 G3
Winkfield Row 5 G4
Winnersh **7,325** 5 F4
Winterbourne **180** 4 B3
Wokefield Park **295** 5 E4
Wokingham **29,424** 5 F4
Wokingham Without **6,568** *
Woodlands Park 5 G3
Woodley **25,339** 5 F3
Woodside 5 G4
Woolhampton **625** 4 D4
World's End 4 C3
Wraysbury **3,544** 5 H3
Yattendon **288** 4 C3

Population figures are based upon the 1991 census and relate to the local authority area or parish as constituted at that date. Places with no population figure form part of a larger local authority area or parish. District boundaries are shown on pages 8-9.

Population figures in bold type.   *Parish not shown on map pages 4-5 due to limitation of scale.

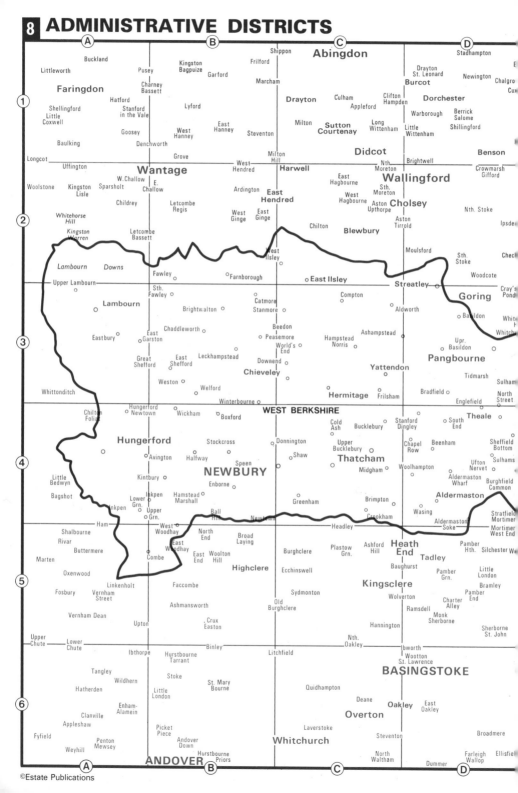

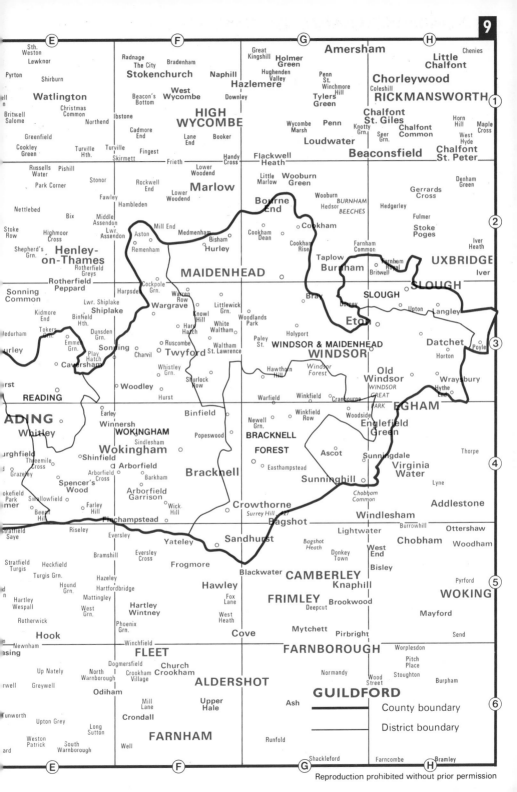

9

Grid references: E, F, G, H (top and bottom), 1, 2, 3, 4, 5, 6 (right side)

Place names visible on the map:

Sth. Weston, Lewknor, Pyrton, Shirburn, Watlington, Britwell Salome, Greenfield, Cookley Green, Turville Hth., Turville, Fingest, Russells Water, Pishill, Park Corner, Nettlebed, Bix, Stoke Row, Highmoor Cross, Shepherd's Grn., Henley-on-Thames, Rotherfield Greys, Rotherfield Peppard, Sonning Common, Kidmore End, Binfield Hth., Tokers Grn., Dunsden Grn., Emmer Grn., Caversham, READING, Whitley

Radnage, The City, Bradnage, Stokenchurch, Naphill, Beacon's Bottom, West Wycombe, Ibstone, Northend, Cadmore End, Lane End, Booker, Christmas Common, Fawley, Hambleden, Middle Assendon, Lwr. Assendon, Mill End, Aston, Remenham, Stonor, Rockwell End, Lower Woodend, Lower Woodend, Marlow, Medmenham, Bisham, Hurley, Frieth, Skirmett, Handy Cross

Great Kingshill, Holmer Green, Hughenden Valley, Downley, Hazlemere, HIGH WYCOMBE, Wycombe Marsh, Penn, Loudwater, Flackwell Heath, Little Marlow, Wooburn Green, Bourne End, Wooburn, Hedsor, BURNHAM BEECHES, Cookham, Cookham Dean, Cookham Rise, Bray, Maidenhead, Cockpole Grn., Harpsden, Warren Row, Wargrave, Lwr. Shiplake, Shiplake, Binfield Hth., Sonning, Charvil, Twyford, Ruscombe, Whistley Grn., Woodley, Hurst, Earley, Winnersh, Sindlesham, Wokingham, WOKINGHAM, Shinfield, Arborfield, Arborfield Cross, Barkham, Bracknell, BRACKNELL FOREST, Easthampstead, Spencer's Wood, Arborfield Garrison, Swallowfield, Farley Hill, Finchampstead, Riseley, Eversley, Yateley, Bramshill, Eversley Cross, Frogmore, Hazeley, Hartfordbridge, Mattingley, West Grn., Hartley Wintney, Phoenix Grn., Hook, Winchfield, FLEET, Up Nately, North Warnborough, Dogmersfield, Crookham Village, Church Crookham, Odiham, Mill Lane, Crondall, Upper Hale, FARNHAM, Well, South Warnborough, Long Sutton, Weston Patrick, Upton Grey, Greywell

Amersham, Chenies, Little Chalfont, Chorleywood, Coleshill, RICKMANSWORTH, Penn St., Winchmore Hill, Tylers Green, Chalfont St. Giles, Knotty Grn., Seer Grn., Chalfont Common, Horn Hill, Maple Cross, West Hyde, Chalfont St. Peter, Beaconsfield, Gerrards Cross, Denham Green, Hedgerley, Fulmer, Stoke Poges, Iver Heath, Taplow, Burnham, Farnham Common, Farnham Royal, Britwell, UXBRIDGE, Iver, SLOUGH, Upton, Langley, Eton, Dorney, Holyport, Paley St., WINDSOR & MAIDENHEAD, WINDSOR, Bray, Hawthorn Hill, Windsor Forest, Old Windsor, Datchet, Poyle, Horton, Wraysbury, Hythe End, WINDSOR GREAT PARK, EGHAM, Warfield, Winkfield, Cranbourne, Woodside, Englefield Green, Binfield, Newell Grn., Popeswood, Winkfield Row, Ascot, Sunningdale, Virginia Water, Thorpe, Lyne, Sunninghill, Chobham Common, Addlestone, Crowthorne, Surrey Hill, Bagshot, Windlesham, Lightwater, Burrowhill, Ottershaw, Sandhurst, Bagshot Heath, Donkey Town, West End, Chobham, Woodham, Blackwater, CAMBERLEY, Bisley, Pyrford, WOKING, Hawley, Fox Lane, Knaphill, FRIMLEY, Brookwood, Deepcut, Mayford, Cove, West Heath, Mytchett, Pirbright, Send, FARNBOROUGH, Worplesdon, Pitch Place, Stoughton, Burpham, Normandy, Wood Street, ALDERSHOT, Ash, GUILDFORD, Runfold, Shackleford, Farncombe, Bramley

County boundary
District boundary

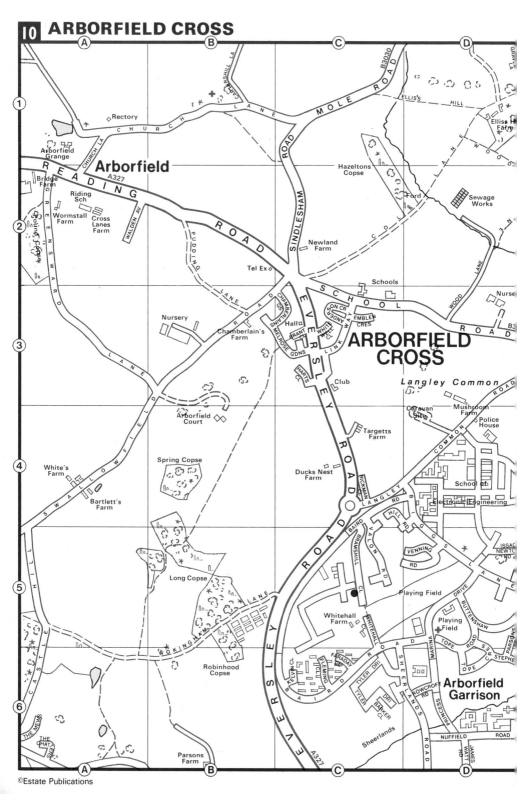

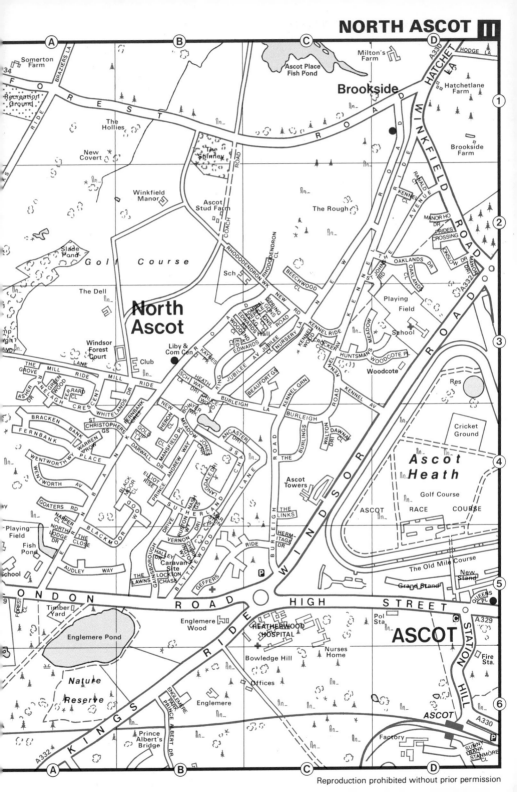

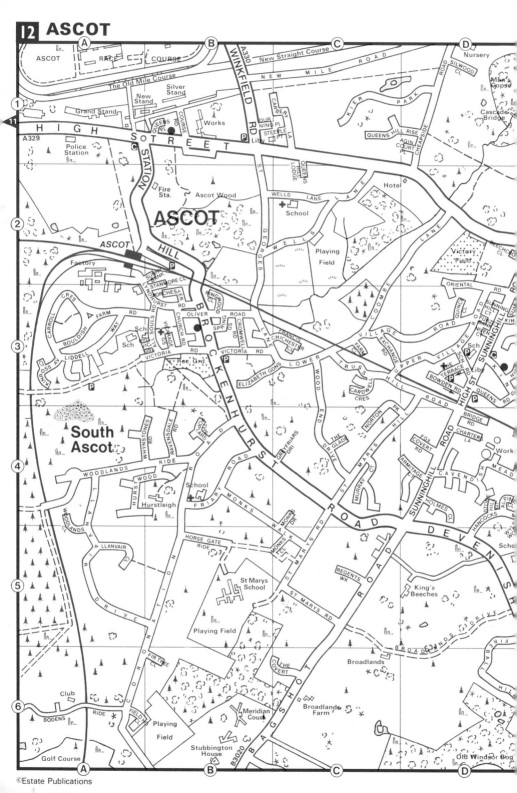

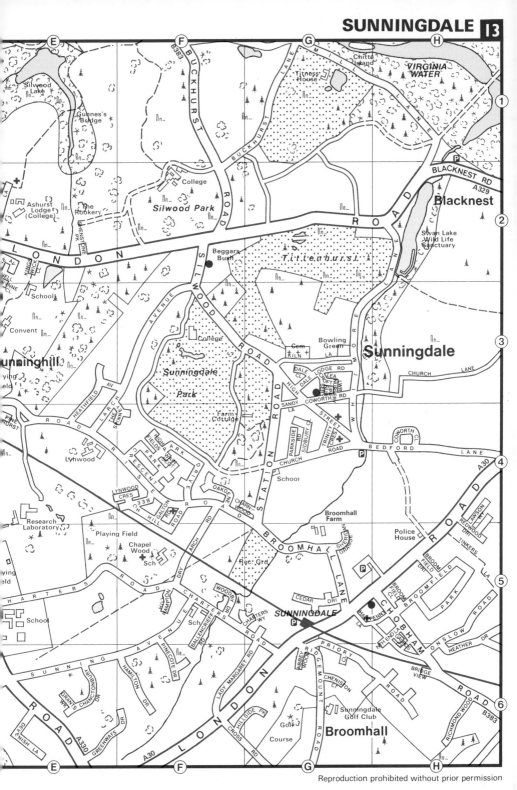

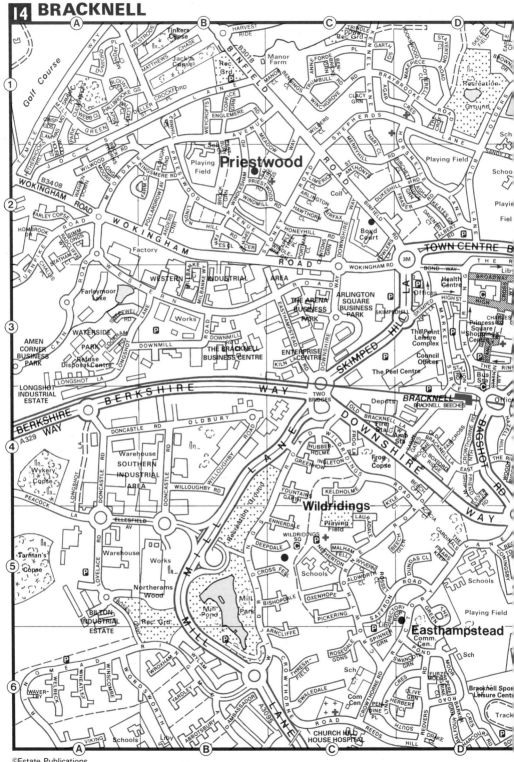

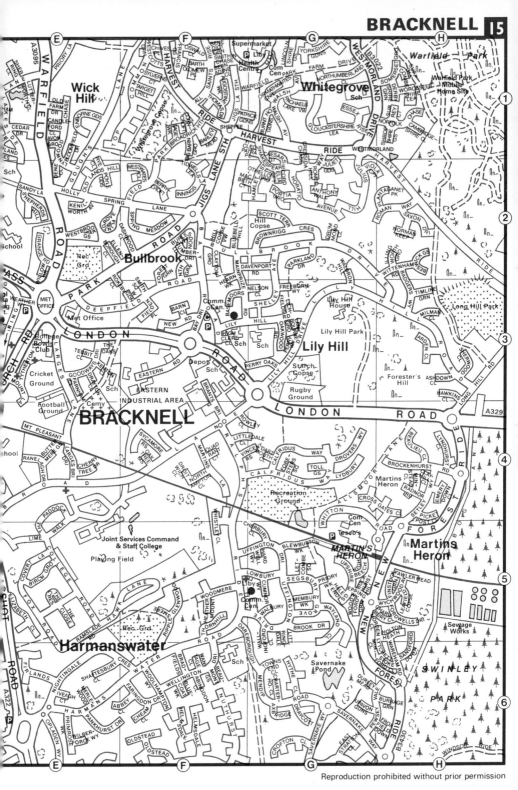

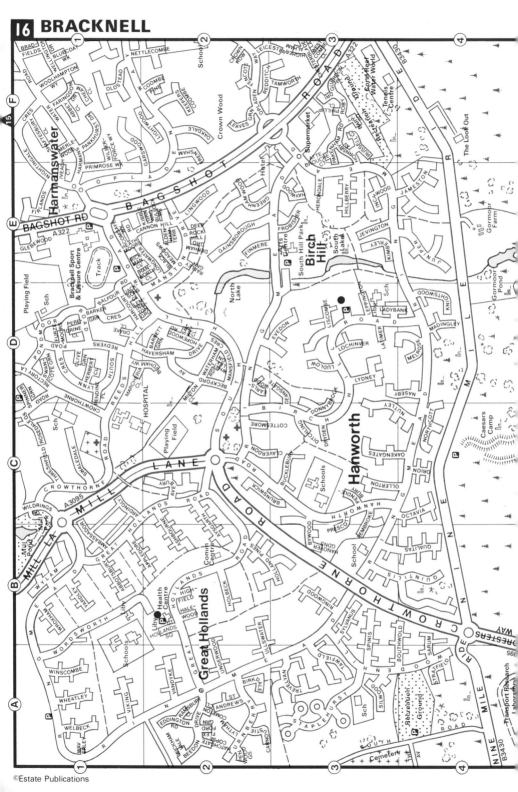

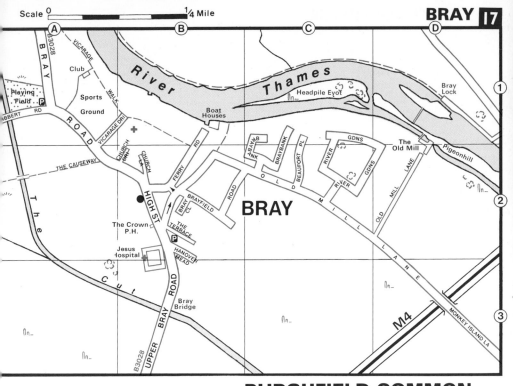

Scale 0 — ¼ Mile

BRAY

BURGHFIELD COMMON

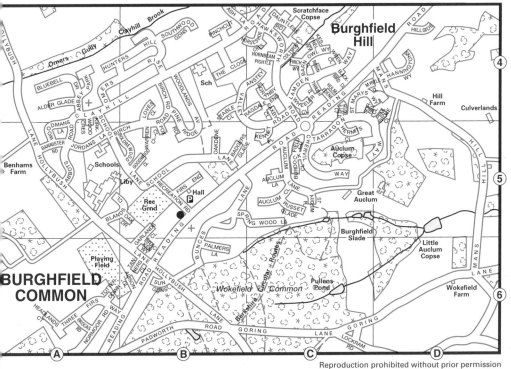

BURGHFIELD COMMON

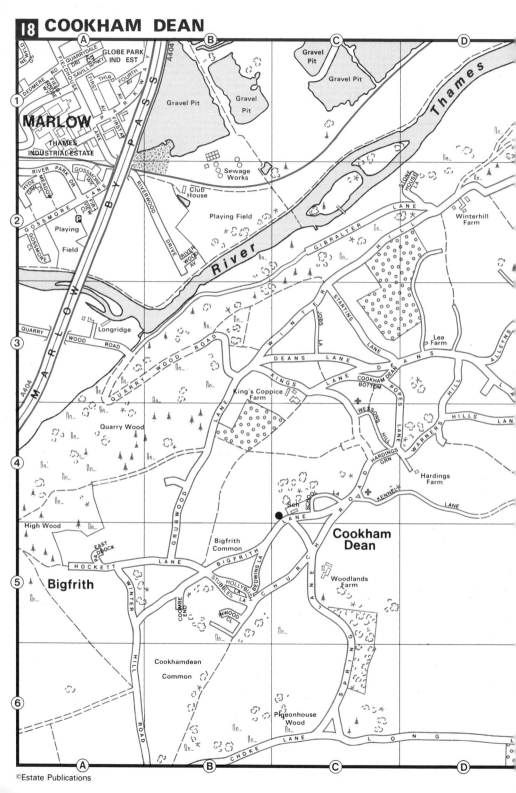

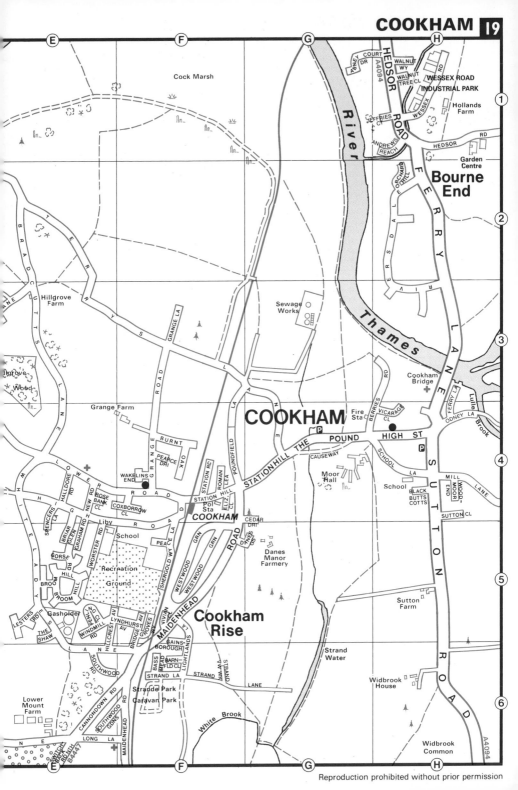

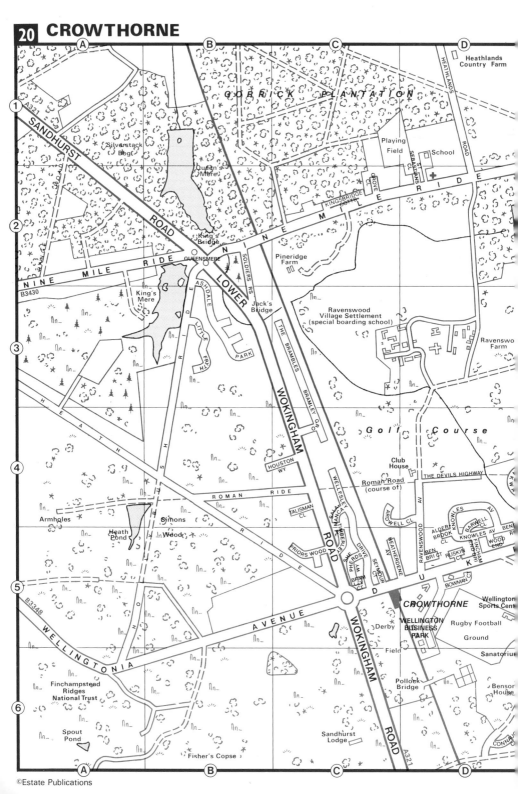

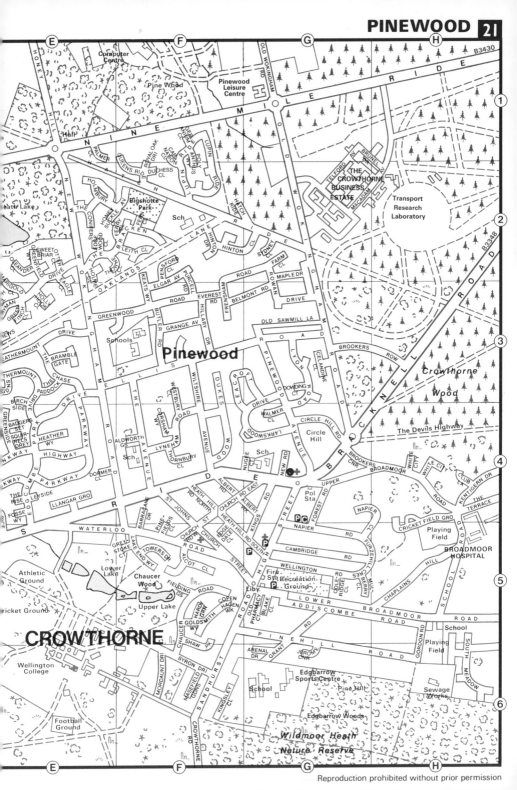

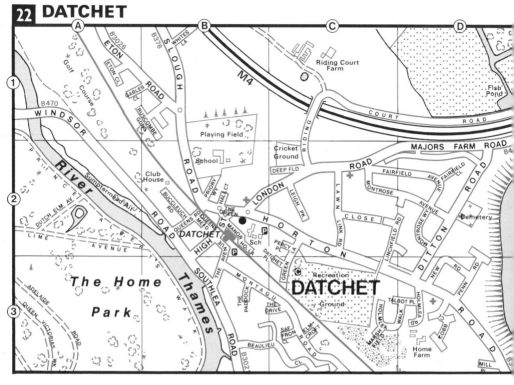

LAMBOURN

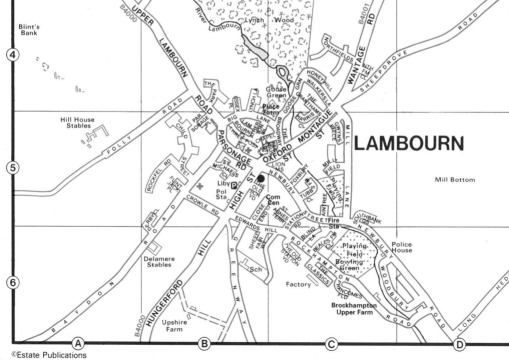

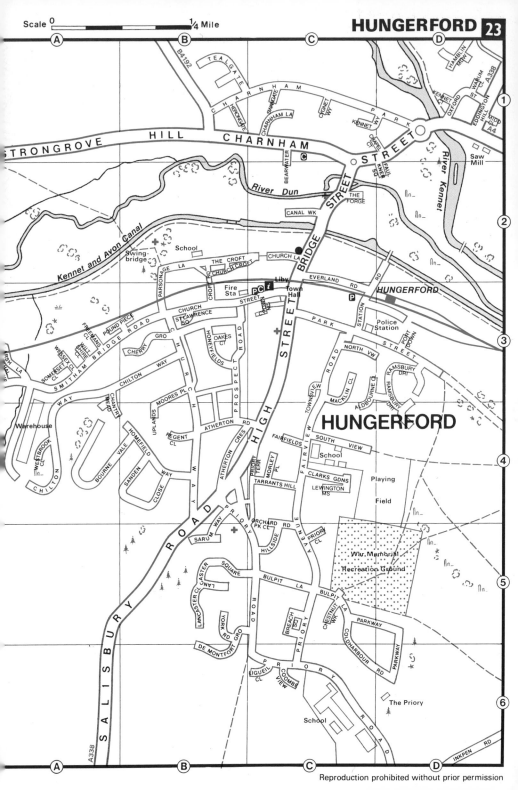

Scale 0 ¼ Mile

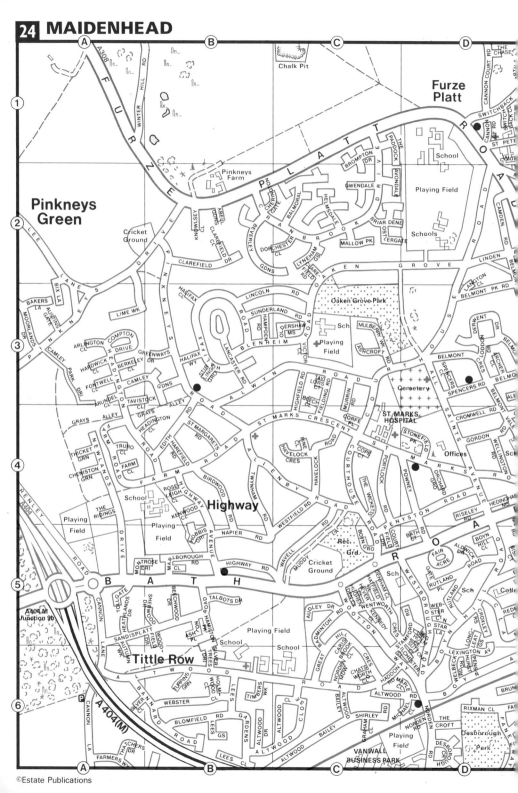

Pinkneys Green

Furze Platt

Tittle Row

Highway

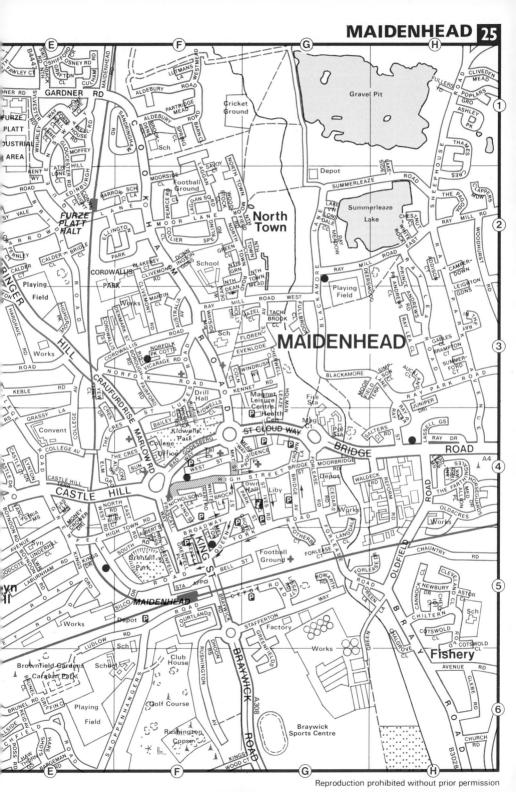

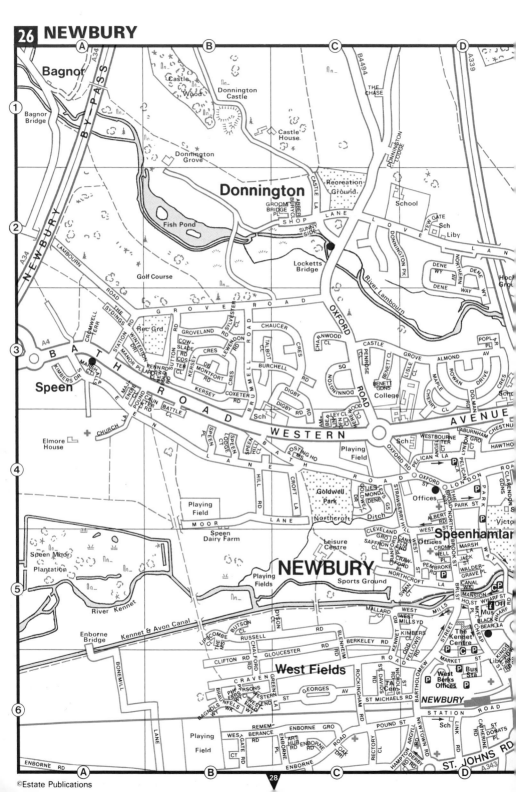

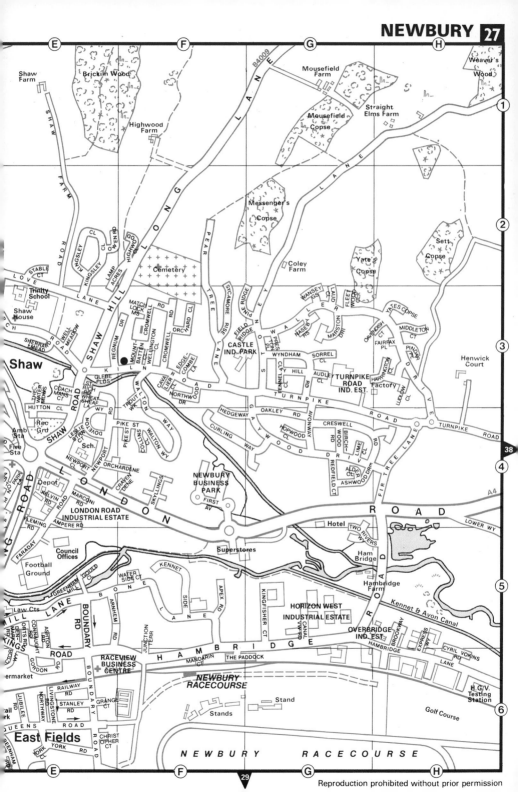

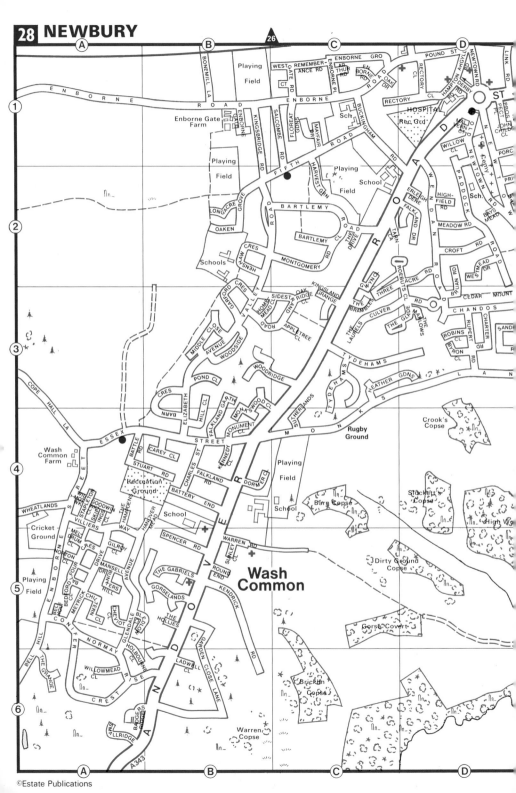

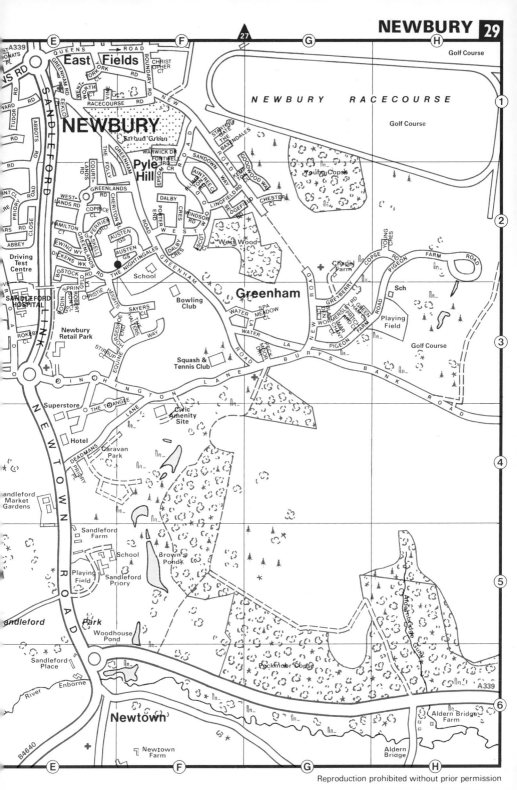

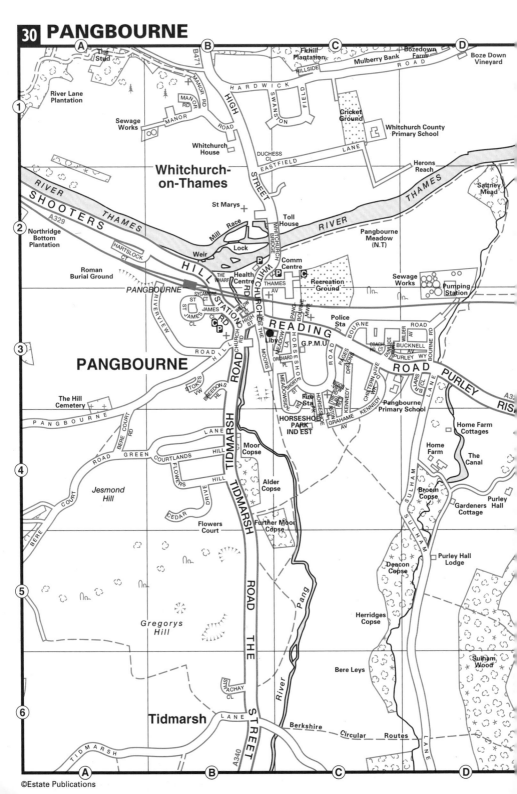

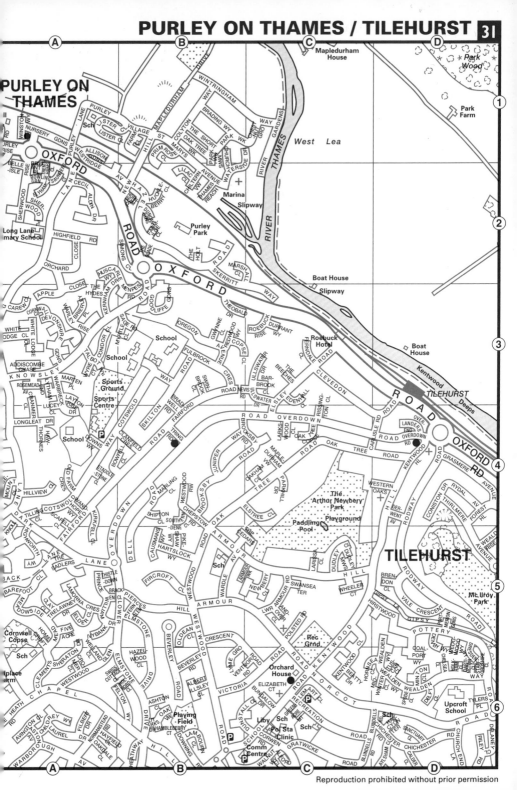

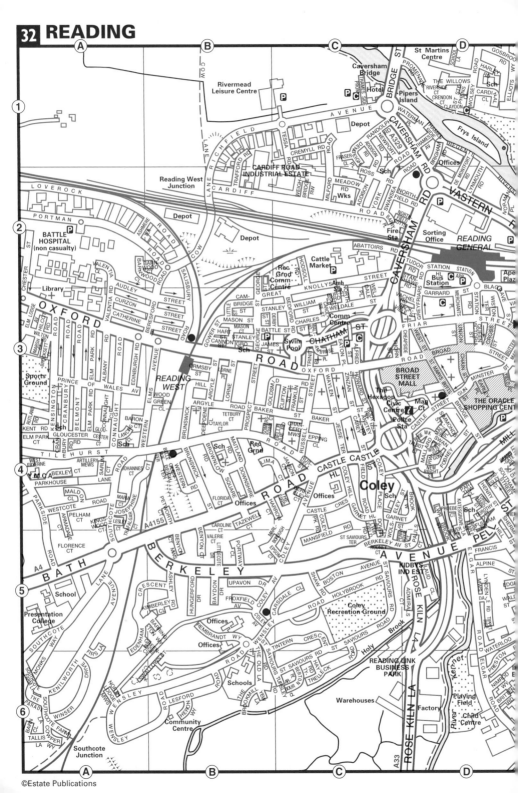

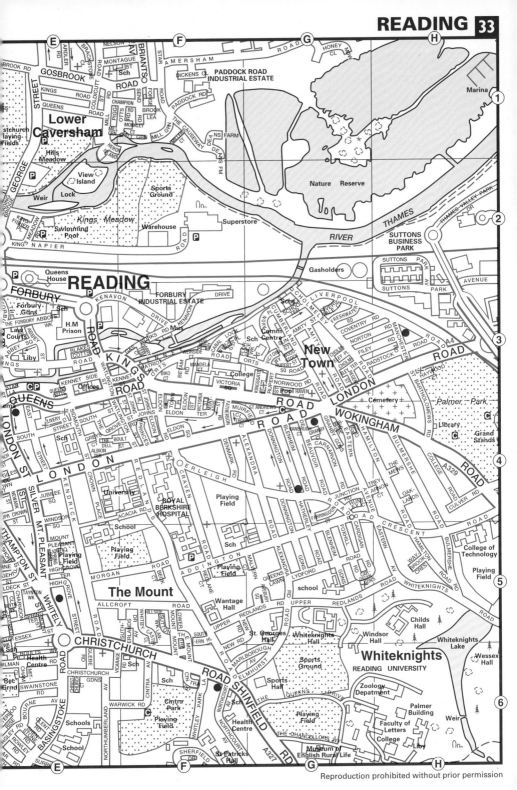

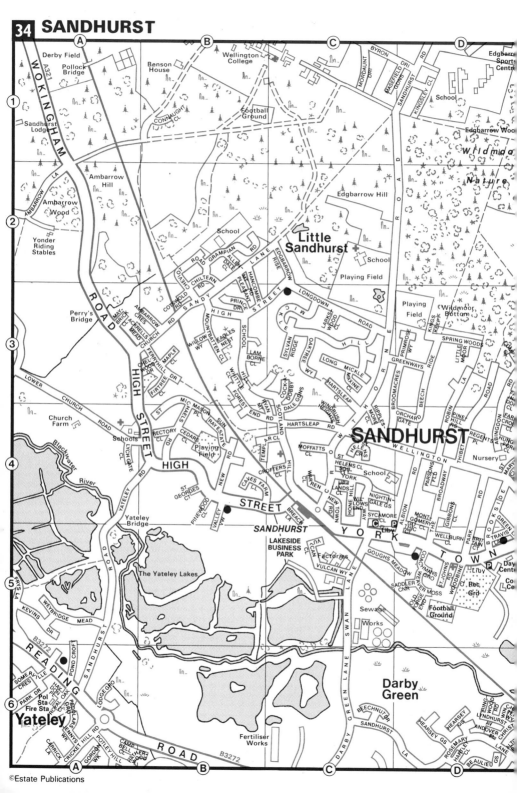

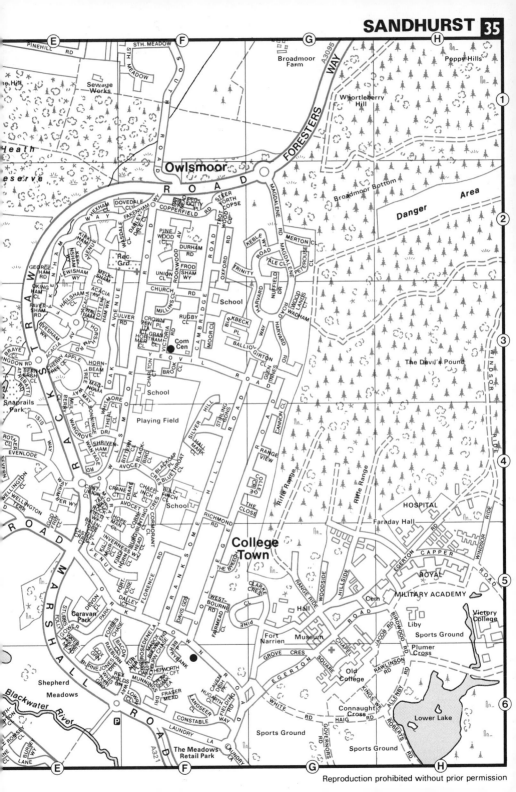

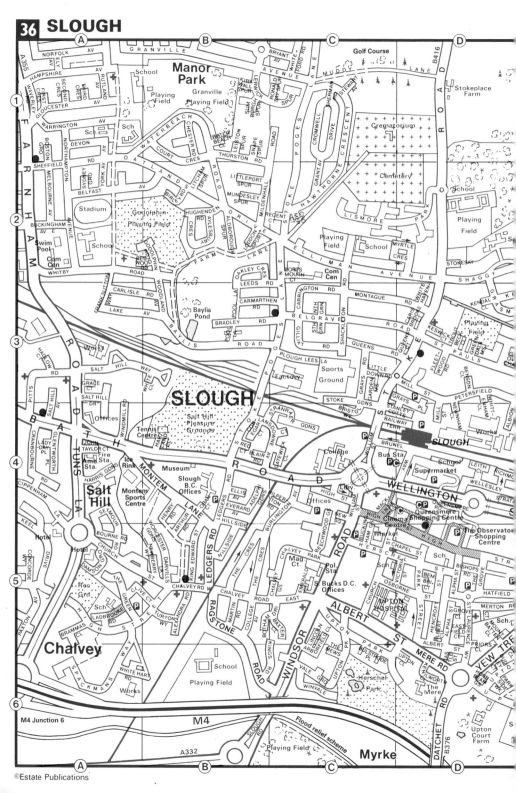

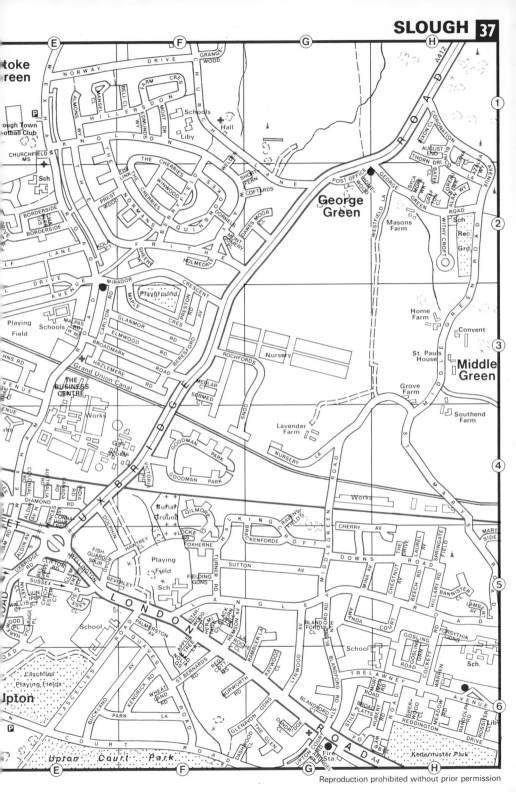

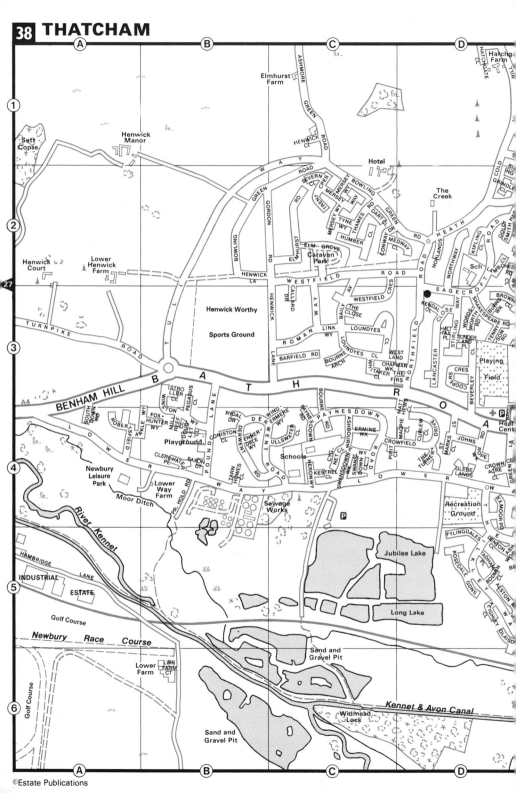

A   B   C   D

1

Seft Copse

Henwick Manor

Elmhurst Farm

HATCHGATE CL

Hatchg Farm

Hotel

The Creek

COLD

BING

GRINDLE

2

Henwick Court

Lower Henwick Farm

WAY

GORDON ROAD

BOWLING RD

HENWICK LA

HENWICK

SEVERN CL

TRENT RD

MERSEY WY

MERSEY WY

TYNE WY

HUMBER CL

THAMES CL

CONWAY CL

MEDWAY CL

DART CL

BOWLING GREEN RD

NORLANDS

HEATH ROAD

NORTHWAY

KIPLING

COLD SMITH

SCH

TANBCHES RD

BROWN

27

Henwick Worthy

Sports Ground

WESTFIELD

ROMAN

ELM

ELMHURST CL

GROVE

Caravan Park

CALLARD DR

HENWICK

BAILY AV

WESTFIELD CRES

THE CLOSE

WEST LAND

ROAD

LINK WY

LOUNDYES

LOUNDYES CL

LANCASTER

SAGECROFT

KENDAL CL

CLOSE

STIRLING

SHAKESPEARE RD

WORDS WORTH PL

HALL FAX PL

SUNDER LAND

BROWN

BK CL

3

TURNPIKE ROAD

A4

Henwick Court

LANE

BARFIELD RD

BOURNE

ARCH

CHAPMAN WK

WTAKER CL

THE FIRS

THE

COOPER CRES

BEVERLEY

Playing Field

4

BENHAM HILL

SOUTH DOWN RD

ROBERTS

KYLE WY

WINS LOW

CLEREWAT PL

STRO LLER CL

PEGASUS CL

FOX HUNTER WY

REEF WY

DOUBLET

SAXON CT

POUND LANE

RYDAL DR

CONISTON CL

TARN HOWES CL

DERWENT

ERMERE

ULLSWATER CL

DERWENT RD

DENNER DALE WY

WIND

WY

BOURNE RD

PAYNE SDOWN RD

PAYNESDOWN

ASHBOURN

HERON WY

KESTREL CL

SWAN CL

NET CL

SWINDOWN WY

SWANS DOWN

CL

ERMINE WK

PIPIT CL

CROWFIELD

MAGPIE CL

CURLEW

THE TURNERY

MATT HEWS

MARKS CL

DRIVE

JOHNS RD

GLEBE LANDS

ROPE

ROAD

CROWN ACRE CL

GREEN LA

Heal Cent

P

Newbury Leisure Park

Playground

Schools

Lower Way Farm

Moor Ditch

PR. HOLD RD

River Kennel

Sewage Works

P

Recreation Ground

FYLINGDALES

DENTON RD

EX MOOR RD

ROSEDALE GDNS

LADNAM

BODR

ALSTON CL

KEIGHLEY CL

5

INDUSTRIAL ESTATE

HAMBRIDGE LANE

Golf Course

Jubilee Lake

Long Lake

GLAISD

6

Golf Course

Newbury   Race   Course

Lower Farm

LWR FARM CT

Sand and Gravel Pit

Kennet & Avon Canal

Widmead Lock

Sand and Gravel Pit

A   B   C   D

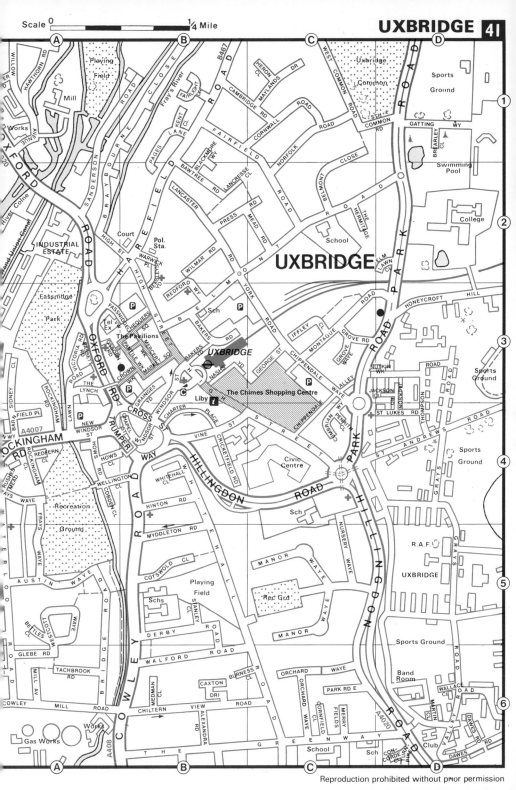

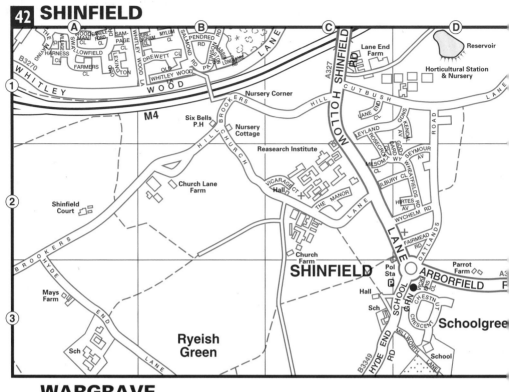

WARGRAVE

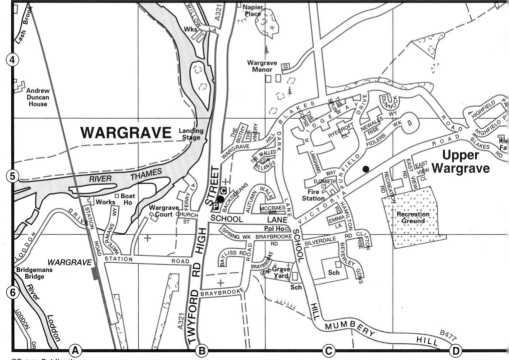

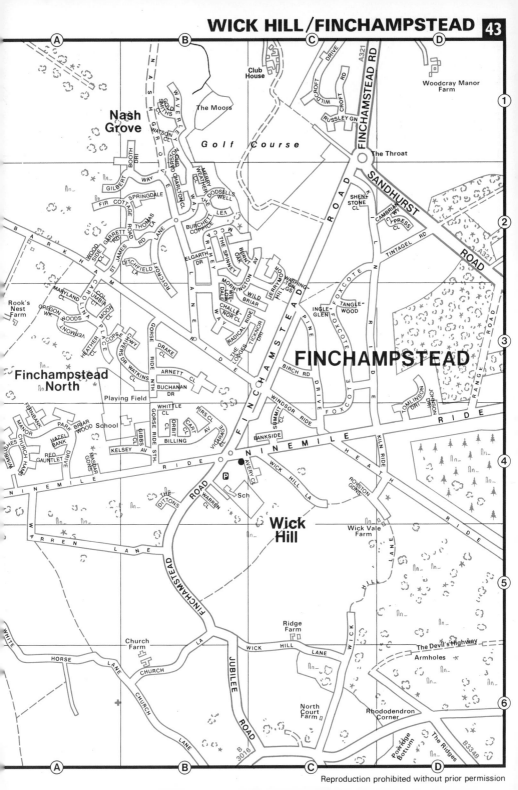

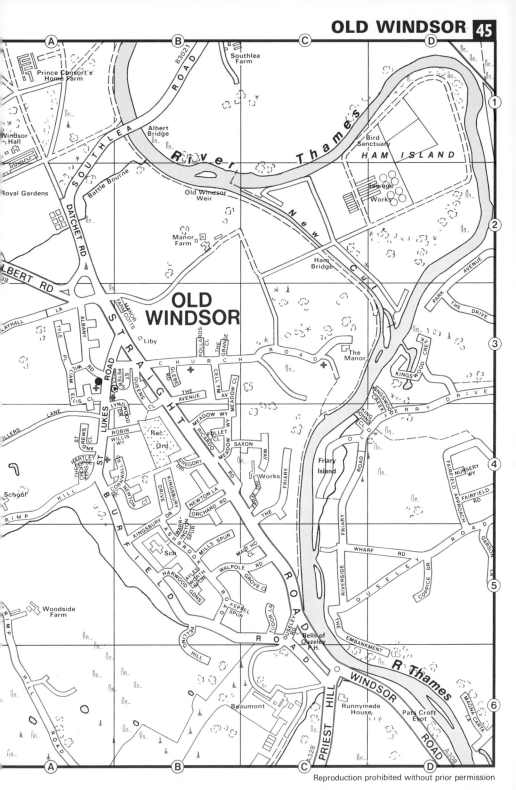

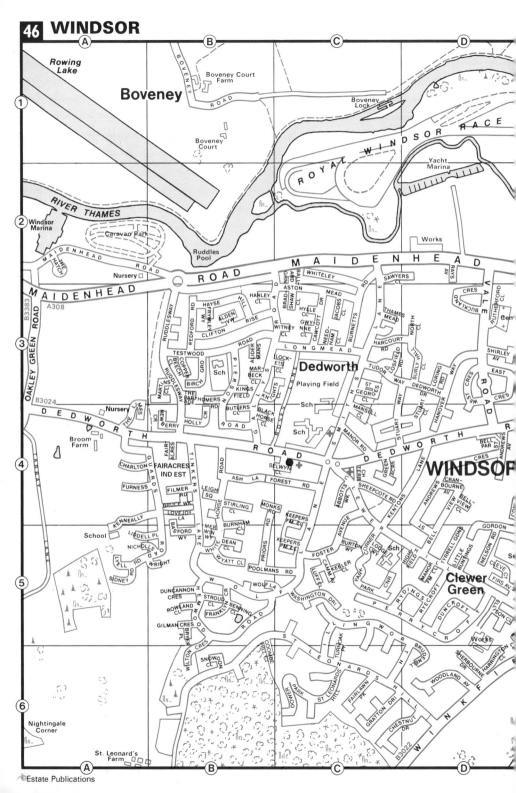

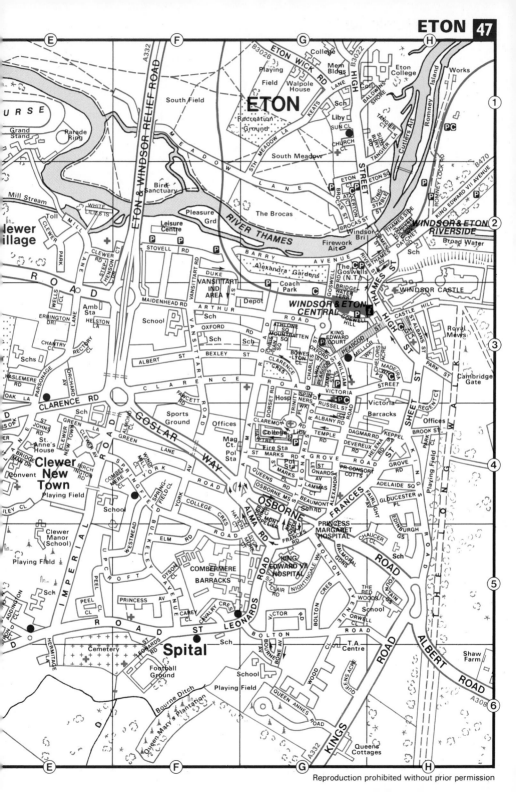

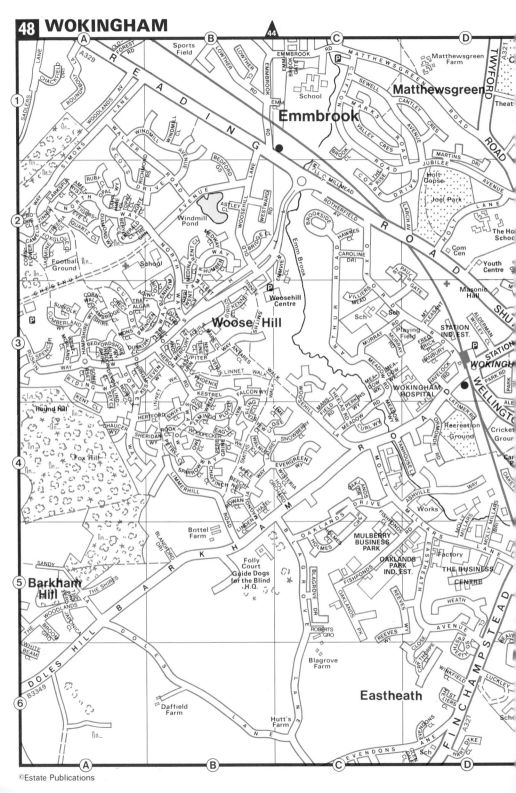

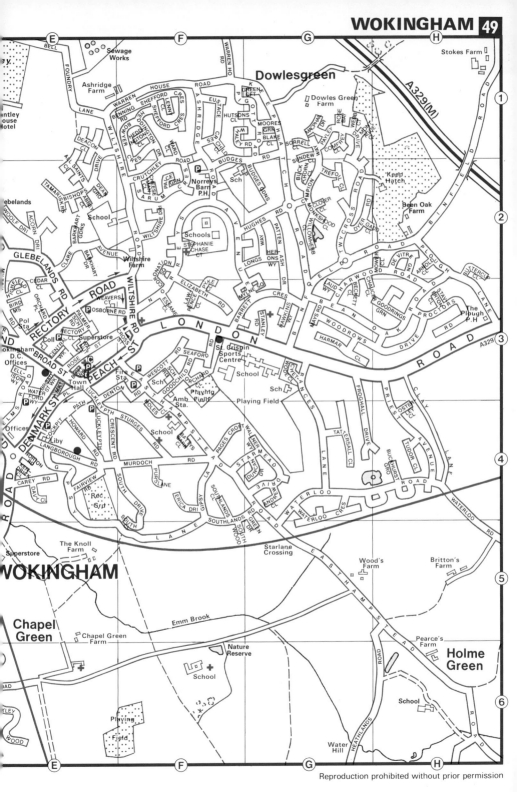

A - Z INDEX TO STREETS
with Postcodes

The Index includes some names for which there is insufficient space on the maps. These names are preceded by an * and are followed by the nearest adjoining thoroughfare.

ARBORFIELD CROSS

Anderson Cres. RG2 10 C3
Baird Rd. RG2 10 C6
Barker Clo. RG2 10 C6
Biggs La. RG2 10 D4
Bramshill Clo. RG2 10 C5
Brant Clo. RG2 10 C5
Buttenshaw Av. RG2 10 D5
Cartershill La. RG2 10 B1
Castle Hill. RG2 10 A6
Chamberlains Gdns.
  RG2 10 C3
Church La. RG2 10 A2
Cole La. RG2 10 C2
Ellis's Hill. RG2 10 C1
Emblen Cres. RG2 10 C3
Eversley Rd. RG2 10 C3
Faraday Rd. RG2 10 C6
Fleming Clo. RG2 10 C6
Gravelpithill La. RG2 10 D1
Greensward La. RG2 10 A2
Harts Clo. RG2 10 C4
Isaac Newton Rd. RG2 10 D5
James Watt Rd. RG2 10 D6
Kelvin Clo. RG2 10 C6
Langley Common Rd.
  RG2 10 C4
Link Way. RG2 10 C3
Melrose Gdns. RG2 10 B3
Mole Rd. RG2 10 C1
Nuffield Rd. RG2 10 D6
Parsons Clo. RG2 10 D6
Princess Marina Dri.
  RG2 10 D6
Pudding La. RG2 10 B2
Reading Rd. RG2 10 A2
Rickman Clo. RG2 10 C4
Rowcroft Rd. RG2 10 D6
School Rd. RG2 10 C3
Sheerlands Rd. RG2 10 C6
Sindlesham Rd. RG2 10 C2
Stephenson Rd. RG2 10 D6
Swallowfield Rd. RG2 10 A4
The Chatters. RG2 10 A6
The Mews. RG2 10 A6
Tope Cres. RG2 10 D6
Tope Rd. RG2 10 D5
Tyler Dri. RG2 10 C6
Valon Rd. RG2 10 C5
Venning Rd. RG2 10 D5
Walden Av. RG2 10 A2
Whitehall Clo. RG2 10 C5
Whitewell Clo. RG2 10 C3
Wokingham La. RG2 10 B6
Wood La. RG2 10 D3

ASCOT

Abbey Wood. SL5 13 G6
Admiral Kepple Ct. SL5 11 C3
Agincourt Pl. SL5 12 D1
All Souls Rd. SL5 12 B3
Alpine Clo. SL5 12 D4
Ancaster Dri. SL5 11 B4
Armitage Ct. SL5 12 D4
Asher Dri. SL5 11 A3
Audley Way. SL5 11 A5
Bagshot Rd. SL5 12 B6
Ballencrieff Rd. SL5 13 F5
Beaufort Gdns. SL5 11 C5
Bedford La. SL5 13 G4
Beech Hill Rd. SL5 13 G6
Beechcroft Clo. SL5 12 D2
Beechwood Clo. SL5 11 C3

Blackmoor Clo. SL5 11 B4
Blackmoor Wood. SL5 11 A5
Blacknest Rd. SL5 13 H2
Blythewood La. SL5 11 B5
Bodens Ride. SL5 12 A6
Bouldish Farm Rd. SL5 12 A3
Bowden Rd. SL5 12 D3
Bowyer Wk. SL5 11 B4
Bracken Bank. SL5 11 A4
Braziers La. RG42 11 A1
Bridge Rd. SL5 12 D4
Bridge Vw. SL5 13 H6
Broadlands Dri. SL5 12 C5
Brockenhurst Rd. SL5 12 B3
Broomfield Clo. SL5 13 H5
Broomfield Dri. SL5 13 H5
Broomfield Pk. SL5 13 H5
Broomhall La. SL5 13 G5
Buckhurst La. SL5 13 F1
Buckhurst Rd. SL5 13 F1
Burleigh La. SL5 11 B3
Burleigh Rd. SL5 11 C4
Carbery La. SL5 12 C1
Cardwell Cres. SL5 12 C3
Carroll Cres. SL5 12 A3
Cavendish Meads. SL5 12 D4
Cedar Dri. SL5 13 G5
Chanctonbury Dri. SL5 13 E6
Charnwood. SL5 13 G4
Charters La. SL5 12 D4
Charters Rd. SL5 13 E5
Charters Way. SL5 13 G5
Cheapside Rd. SL5 12 D1
Cheniston Ct. SL5 13 G6
Cherrington Way. SL5 11 B5
Chobham Rd. SL5 13 H5
Church La,
  Sunningdale. SL5 13 H3
Church La,
  Sunninghill. SL5 13 E2
Church Rd, Ascot. SL5 12 B3
Church Rd,
  Sunningdale. SL5 13 G4
Coach Rd. SL5 11 B2
Coombe La. SL5 12 C3
Coronation Rd. SL5 12 A6
Course Rd. SL5 12 B1
Coworth Cres. SL5 13 H4
Coworth Rd. SL5 13 G3
Crocker Clo. SL5 11 C3
Cromwell Rd. SL5 12 B3
Cross Rd. SL5 13 F6
Dale Clo. SL5 13 G3
Dale Lodge Rd. SL5 13 G3
Darwall Dri. SL5 11 B4
Dawnay Clo. SL5 11 C4
Devenish La. SL5 13 E6
Devenish Rd. SL5 12 D5
Druce Wood. SL5 11 B3
Dry Arch Rd. SL5 13 F5
Durning Pl. SL5 12 B1
Elizabeth Gdns. SL5 12 B3
Elliot Rise. SL5 11 B4
Englemere Park. SL5 11 B6
Exchange Rd. SL5 12 C3
Farm Clo. SL5 12 C3
Fernbank Cres. SL5 11 B4
Fernbank Pl. SL5 11 A4
Fernbank Rd. SL5 11 A5
Ferrard Clo. SL5 11 A3
Field House Clo. SL5 12 A6
Fir Tree Clo. SL5 12 B6
Fireball Hill. SL5 12 D5
Forest Clo. SL5 11 A5
Forest Rd. SL5 11 A1
Fox Covert Rd. SL5 12 D4
Francis Chichester Clo.
  SL5 12 C3
Friary Rd. SL5 12 B4
Furzebank. SL5 12 D3
Gainsborough Dri. SL5 11 B5
Galton Rd. SL5 13 F4
Geffers Ride. SL5 11 B5
Goaters Rd. SL5 11 A4
Gold Cup La. SL5 11 B4
Grants Walk. SL5 13 E6
Green Wood. SL5 11 A3
Greenways Dri. SL5 13 E6

Greyfriars Dri. SL5 12 C4
Guards Ct. SL5 13 H5
Halfpenny La. SL5 13 G5
Halley Dri. SL5 11 B5
Hamilton Dri. SL5 13 F6
Hancocks Mt. SL5 12 D5
Hatchet La. SL5 11 D1
Heather Dri. SL5 13 H6
Heathfield Av. SL5 13 E4
Heathway Dri. SL5 11 B3
Hermitage Dri. SL5 11 C5
Heron Clo. SL5 11 B4
High Fields. SL5 13 F4
High St, Ascot. SL5 11 C5
High St,
  Sunningdale. SL5 13 G3
High St,
  Sunninghill. SL5 12 D3
Highclere. SL5 12 D3
Hillhampton. SL5 13 F5
Hillside Pk. SL5 13 F6
Hodge La. SL4 11 D1
Holmes Clo. SL5 12 D4
Horse Gate Ride. SL5 12 B5
Huntsmans Meadow.
  SL5 11 C3
Hurstwood. SL5 12 A4
Jones Cnr. SL5 11 B4
Jubilee Av. SL5 11 B3
Jubilee Clo. SL5 11 C3
Kaynes Pk. SL5 11 B3
Kennel Av. SL5 11 C3
Kennel Clo. SL5 11 D2
Kennel Grn. SL5 11 C3
Kennel Ride. SL5 11 C3
Kennel Wood. SL5 11 C3
Kier Pk. SL5 12 C1
Kiln La. SL5 13 G3
King Edwards Clo. SL5 11 B3
King Edwards Rise. SL5 11 C3
King Edwards Rd. SL5 11 B3
Kings Ride. SL5 11 A6
Kings Rd. SL5 12 D3
Kingswick Clo. SL5 13 E2
Kingswick Dri. SL5 12 D3
Kinross Av. SL5 12 A3
Kinross Ct. SL5 12 A3
Lady Margaret Rd. SL5 13 F6
Langdale Dri. SL5 11 B4
Larch Av. SL5 13 E4
Lawson Way. SL5 13 H4
Leacroft. SL5 13 G3
Liddell Way. SL5 12 A3
Llanvair Clo. SL5 12 A4
Llanvair Dri. SL5 11 A4
Locks Ride. SL5 11 A2
Lockton Chase. SL5 11 B5
London Rd,
  Burleigh. SL5 11 A5
London Rd
  Sunningdale. SL5 13 F6
London Rd,
  Sunninghill. SL5 13 E2
Lower Nursery. SL5 13 G3
Lower Village Rd. SL5 12 C3
Lyndhurst Rd. SL5 12 A3
Lynwood Cres. SL5 13 F4
Manor Dri. SL5 11 D2
Manor House Dri. SL5 11 D2
Mansfield Clo. SL5 11 B4
Mansfield Pl. SL5 11 B4
Marston Way. SL5 11 B4
Mill La. SL5 13 G1
Mill Ride. SL5 11 A3
Monks Clo. SL5 12 C5
Monks Dri. SL5 12 C4
Monks Walk. SL5 12 B4
Murray Ct. SL5 12 C4
Napper Clo. SL5 11 A4
Nash Gdns. SL5 11 B4
Nell Gwynne Av. SL5 13 E2
Nell Gwynne Clo. SL5 13 E2
New Meadow. SL5 11 B4
New Mile Rd. SL5 12 B1
New Rd. SL5 12 D3
Niven Ct. SL5 12 D3
North End La. SL5 13 H5
North Lodge Dri. SL5 11 A5

Norton Pk. SL5 12 C4
Nursery La. SL5 11 C3
Oakdene. SL5 13 F4
Oaklands Clo. SL5 11 D2
Oaklands Dri. SL5 11 D2
Oliver Rd. SL5 12 B3
Onslow Dri. SL5 11 D2
Onslow Rd. SL5 13 H6
Oriental Rd. SL5 12 D2
Park Cres. SL5 13 F4
Park Dri. SL5 13 F4
Parkside Rd. SL5 13 G4
Pembroke Clo. SL5 12 D4
Pinecote Dri. SL5 13 F6
Pinehurst. SL5 13 E4
Porchester. SL5 12 B3
Prides Crossing. SL5 12 B2
Prince Albert Dri. SL5 11 B6
Prince Andrew Way.
  SL5 11 B4
Priory Clo. SL5 13 G6
Priory Rd. SL5 13 G6
Queens Clo. SL5 11 C3
Queens Hill Rise. SL5 12 D1
Queenshill Lodge. SL5 12 C2
Queens Pl. SL5 11 D5
Queens Rd. SL5 12 D3
Quince Clo. SL5 12 D3
Ranald Ct. SL5 11 D2
Ranelagh Cres. SL5 11 A3
Ravensdale Rd. SL5 12 B4
Redwood Dri. SL5 13 H5
Regents Walk. SL5 12 C5
Rhododendron Clo. SL5 11 C2
Rhododendron Walk.
  SL5 11 B2
Richmond Wood. SL5 11 B4
Ridgemount Rd. SL5 13 G6
Ringwood Clo. SL5 12 B3
Rise Rd. SL5 13 E4
Royal Victoria Gdns.
  SL5 12 A3
Ruston Way. SL5 11 B4
St Christophers Gdns.
  SL5 11 A4
St Georges La. SL5 12 B2
St Johns Rd. SL5 11 D2
St Marys Hill. SL5 12 C4
St Marys Rd. SL5 12 C5
Sandy La,
  North Ascot. SL5 11 A3
Sandy La,
  Sunningdale. SL5 13 G4
School La. SL5 11 B3
School Rd. SL5 12 D3
Shenstone Pk. SL5 13 E2
Sheridan Grange. SL5 11 B4
Sidbury Clo. SL5 13 G4
Silwood Clo. SL5 12 D1
Silwood Rd. SL5 13 F2
Spring Gdns,
  Nth Ascot. SL5 11 C3
Spring Gdns,
  Sth Ascot. SL5 12 B3
Stanmore Clo. SL5 12 B2
Station Hill. SL5 11 D5
Station Rd. SL5 13 G4
Steeple Point. SL5 12 B1
Stonehill Gate. SL5 12 D4
Sunning Av. SL5 13 E6
Sunninghill Clo. SL5 12 D3
Sunninghill Ct. SL5 12 D3
Sunninghill Rd. SL5 12 D3
Sunnybank. SL5 12 B2
Sutherland Chase. SL5 11 A4
Tenby Dri. SL5 13 E4
The Avenue. SL5 11 D2
The Burlings. SL5 11 C4
The Close. SL5 11 A5
The Covert. SL5 12 C6
The Glade. SL5 12 C4
The Grove. SL5 11 A3
The Lawns. SL5 11 B5
The Links. SL5 11 C5
The Poplars. SL5 12 B4
The Spinney. SL5 13 E4
The Terrace. SL5 12 D3
Tinkers La. SL5 13 H5

Trinity Cres. SL5 13 G4
Truss Hill Rd. SL5 12 C3
Upper Nursery. SL5 13 G3
Upper Village Rd. SL5 12 C3
Vernon Dri. SL5 11 B5
Vicarage Gdns. SL5 11 C5
Victoria Rd. SL5 12 B3
Wainscot. SL5 13 F4
Walton Dri. SL5 11 C4
Warren Row. SL5 11 A4
Wells La. SL5 12 C2
Wentworth Av. SL5 11 A4
Wentworth Way. SL5 11 A4
Whitelands Dri. SL5 11 A4
Whitmore La. SL5 13 G4
Whynstones Rd. SL5 12 A4
Windsor Rd. SL5 11 B5
Winkfield Rd. SL5 11 D1
Wood End Rd. SL5 11 C4
Woodby Dri. SL5 13 F5
Woodcote Pl. SL5 11 D3
Woodend Clo. SL5 11 B3
Woodlands Clo. SL5 12 A4
Woodlands Ride. SL5 12 A4
Wyldwoods. SL5 12 D5

BRACKNELL

Abbey Clo. RG12 15 F6
Abbotsbury. RG12 16 B1
Abingdon Clo. RG12 14 D5
Agar Cres. RG42 14 C1
Albert Rd. RG42 14 D2
Aldenham Ter. RG12 16 E2
Aldworth Clo. RG12 14 C5
All Saints Rise. RG42 15 F1
Allsmoor La. RG12 15 G4
Ambassador. RG12 16 B1
Anders Cnr. RG42 14 C2
Anneforde Pl. RG42 14 C1
Anthony Wall. RG42 15 G2
Appledore. RG12 16 B1
Appletree Pl. RG42 14 C2
Apsey Ct. RG42 14 A1
Arden Clo. RG12 15 H3
Ardingly. RG12 16 C1
Arlington Clo. RG42 14 C2
Arncliffe. RG12 14 B6
Ashbourne. RG12 16 B2
Ashdown Clo. RG12 15 H3
Ashridge Grn. RG42 14 D2
Attebrouche Ct. RG12 16 F3
Augustine Walk. RG42 15 F1
Avebury. RG12 16 B2
Avon Gro. RG12 15 E1
Axbridge. RG12 15 G6
Aysgarth. RG12 16 B2
Badgers Way. RG12 15 H3
Bagshot Rd. RG12 14 D4
Balfour Cres. RG12 16 D1
Barker Grn. RG12 15 F1
Barley Mead. RG42 15 F1
Barn Clo. RG12 15 F3
Barnett Grn. RG12 16 D2
Barry Sq. RG12 16 F3
Bartholomew Pl. RG42 15 F1
Basemoors. RG12 15 F3
Bay Dri. RG12 15 F2
Bay Rd. RG12 15 F2
Beaulieu Clo. RG12 15 F6
Beaumont Gdns. RG12 15 F6
Beckford Av. RG12 16 D2
Beech Croft. RG12 14 D4
Beech Glen. RG12 14 D5
Beedon Dri. RG12 16 A2
Benbricke Grn. RG42 14 C1
Benedict Grn. RG42 15 F1
Bennings Grn. RG42 14 C1
Berkshire Way. RG12 14 A4
Bernadine Clo. RG42 15 F1
Berrycroft. RG12 15 F2
Beswick Gdns. RG42 15 F2
Big Barn Gro. RG42 14 B6
Binfield Rd. RG42 15 E2
Birch Gro. RG12 15 E5

Birch Hill Rd. RG12 16 C2
Birchetts Clo. RG42 14 D2
Birkdale. RG12 16 A2
Bishopdale. RG12 14 B5
Black Meadows. RG12 16 E2
Blewburton Walk. RG12 15 G5
Bloomfield Dri. RG12 15 E1
Blount Cres. RG42 14 A1
Blue Coat Walk. RG12 15 F6
Bluebell Hill. RG12 15 F2
Boltons La. RG42 14 A1
Bond Way. RG12 14 D3
Boxford Ridge. RG
RG12 14 D4
Bradfields. RG12 15 F6
Brants Bri. RG12 15 E1
Braybrooke Rd. RG42 14 C1
Broad La. RG12 15 E4
Broadrick Heath. RG42 15 F1
Broadway. RG12 14 D3
Brockenhurst Rd. RG12 15 H4
Brook Dri. RG12 15 G5
Brook Grn. RG42 14 B2
Broome Ct. RG12 14 D4
Brownlow Dri. RG42 14 D1
Brownrigg Cres. RG12 15 G2
Brunswick. RG12 16 C2
Buckhurst Hill. RG12 15 G5
Bucklebury. RG12 16 C3
Buckthorns. RG42 14 A2
Budham Way. RG12 16 D2
Bull La. RG42 14 D2
Bullbrook Dri. RG12 15 F2
Burbage Grn. RG12 15 H6
Burleson Way. RG12 15 F2
Burnham Gro. RG12 15 E1
Burnt House Gdns.
RG42 15 G1
Buttermere Gdns. RG12 15 E4
Bywood. RG12 16 B3
Caesars Gate. RG42 14 A3
Cain Rd. RG12 14 A3
Calfridus Way. RG12 15 G4
Cambridgeshire Clo.
RG42 15 H1
Candleford Clo. RG12 15 E1
Cannon Hill. RG12 16 E1
Carnoustie. RG12 16 A2
Cedar Dri. RG42 15 E1
Challis Pl. RG42 14 A2
Charlbury Clo. RG12 15 H5
Charles Sq. RG42 14 D3
Charterhouse Clo.
RG12 15 G6
Cheam Clo. RG12 15 F6
Cherbury Clo. RG12 15 G5
Cherry Tree Dri. RG12 15 E4
Chesterblade La. RG12 15 F3
Chives Pl. RG42 15 F1
Church Rd. RG12 15 E3
Clacy Grn. RG12 14 C1
Claverdon. RG12 16 C2
Clayhill Clo. RG12 15 H4
Clayton Gro. RG12 15 G1
Cleopatra Pl. RG42 15 G1
Clintons Grn. RG42 14 C2
Clive Grn. RG12 14 D6
College Rd. RG12 15 E5
Compton Clo. RG12 16 A2
Comsaye Walk. RG12 14 D5
Coningsby. RG12 14 D5
Cookham Rd. RG12 14 A3
Coombe Pine. RG12 16 F2
Coppice Grn. RG42 14 B1
Cordelia Croft. RG42 15 F1
Corncroft. RG42 15 F1
Cotterell Clo. RG12 14 D1
Cottesmore. RG12 16 C2
Covert La. RG12 15 E5
Cressida Chase. RG42 15 G1
Crisp Gdns. RG42 14 A1
Crockford Pl. RG42 14 B1
Crofton Clo. RG12 15 G6
Cross Fell. RG12 14 B5
Cross Gates Clo. RG12 15 H4
Crossway. RG12 14 D3
Crown Row. RG12 16 F2
Crowthorne Rd,
Easthampstead. RG12 14 C6
Crowthorne Rd,
Hanworth. RG12 16 B4
Crowthorne Rd Nth.
RG12 14 D4
Culvercroft. RG42 14 A1

Cumberland Dri. RG12 15 F2
Cumnor Way. RG12 15 G5
Dartmouth Clo. RG12 15 G4
Dashwood Clo. RG12 15 F2
Davenport Rd. RG12 15 F2
Daventry Ct. RG42 14 D2
Deansgate. RG12 16 D3
Deer Rock Hill. RG12 16 E2
Deepdale. RG12 14 B5
Deepfield Rd. RG12 15 E3
Deller St. RG42 14 A1
Dene Clo. RG12 15 E2
Denham Gro. RG12 16 E2
Derbyshire Grn. RG42 15 H1
Ditchling. RG12 16 C3
Doncastle Rd. RG12 14 A4
Donnybrook. RG12 16 C3
Downmill Rd. RG12 14 B3
Downshire Way. RG42 14 C4
Drake Clo. RG12 15 F1
Draycott. RG12 15 G6
Drayton Clo. RG12 15 E3
Droitwich Clo. RG12 15 F4
Drovers Way. RG12 15 G4
Drummond Clo. RG12 15 G2
Dryden. RG12 16 C3
Dukeshill Rd. RG42 14 C2
Dundas Clo. RG12 14 D5
Dunford Pl. RG42 14 A1
Durley Mead. RG12 15 G6
Earlcroft. RG42 14 D1
Earlswood. RG12 16 D2
East Stratton Clo. RG12 15 G6
Eastbury Cl. RG42 14 B2
Eastern Rd. RG12 15 F3
Easthampstead Rd.
RG12 14 C3
Eddington Rd. RG12 16 A2
Elizabeth Clo. RG12 15 E5
Ellenborough Clo. RG12 15 E2
Ellesfield Av. RG12 14 A5
Emerydown Clo. RG12 15 H4
Enbourne Gdns. RG12 15 E1
Englemere Rd. RG42 14 B1
Ennerdale. RG12 14 C5
Epping Way. RG12 15 G1
Essex Rise. RG42 15 G1
Evedon. RG12 16 D3
Faircross. RG42 14 C2
Fairfax. RG42 14 B2
Fanes Clo. RG42 14 B2
Faringdon Dri. RG12 15 F6
Farley Copse. RG42 14 A2
Farm Clo. RG42 14 B2
Farnham Clo. RG12 15 E3
Fawler Mead. RG12 15 H5
Fencote. RG42 16 F2
Fernhill Clo. RG42 14 B1
Field Park. RG12 15 F2
Fielden Pl. RG12 15 F3
Finmere. RG12 16 E2
Finstock Grn. RG12 15 H5
Firlands. RG12 15 E6
Flexford Grn. RG12 16 A2
Flintgrove. RG12 15 E2
Folders La. RG42 14 D1
Fordwells Dri. RG12 15 H5
Forest Grn. RG12 15 F2
Foresters Sq. RG12 15 G4
Foresters Way. RG45 16 B4
Fountains Garth. RG12 14 C4
Fowlers La. RG42 14 C2
Fox Rd. RG12 15 E5
Francis Gdns. RG42 15 F1
Fraser Rd. RG12 14 D2
Freeborn Way. RG12 15 G3
Frensham. RG12 16 F2
Friars Keep. RG12 16 E3
Friendship Way. RG12 14 D4
Frobisher. RG12 16 E3
Frog La. RG12 14 C4
Froxfield Down. RG12 15 H6
Furze Moors. RG12 14 D6
Gainsborough. RG12 16 E2
Garswood. RG12 16 E2
Garth Sq. RG42 14 C1
Glebewood. RG12 14 D6
Glenwood. RG12 15 F5
Gloucestershire Lea.
RG42 15 G1
Goodways Dri. RG12 15 E3
Gough's La. RG12 15 E2
Grange Rd. RG12 15 E2
Great Hollands Rd.
RG12 16 A2

Great Hollands Sq.
RG12 16 B1
Greenham Wood.
RG12 16 E2
Greenhow. RG12 14 C4
Guerdon Pl. RG12 16 F3
Hale End. RG12 15 G5
Halewood. RG12 16 B2
Hallbrooke Gdns. RG42 14 A1
Hamlet St. RG42 15 G2
Hanworth Clo. RG12 16 E1
Hanworth Rd. RG12 16 C3
Hanover Gdns. RG12 16 B3
Harcourt Rd. RG12 16 D1
Hardwell Way. RG12 15 G5
Harmans Water Rd.
RG12 15 E6
Hart Clo. RG42 14 C2
Harvest Rise. RG42 14 B1
Harvest Ride. RG42 15 F1
Hatchgate Copse. RG12 16 A2
Haversham Dri. RG12 16 D1
Hawk La. RG12 15 E5
Hawkins Clo. RG12 15 H3
Hawthorn Clo. RG42 14 C2
Haywood. RG12 16 E3
Hazell Hill. RG12 14 D4
Hearn Walk. RG12 15 F2
Heath Moors. RG12 15 E1
Heathermount. RG12 15 F5
Helmsdale. RG12 15 F6
Herbert Clo. RG12 14 C6
Herondale. RG12 15 G5
High Beech. RG12 14 D3
High St. RG12 14 D4
Highclere Clo. RG12 15 F3
Higher Alham. RG12 15 F3
Highfield. RG12 16 B2
Highfield Clo. RG12 15 F2
Hillberry. RG12 16 C3
Hill Copse Vw. RG12 15 F2
Hitherhooks Hill. RG42 14 A2
Holbeck. RG12 16 B2
Holland Pines. RG12 16 B2
Holly Spring La. RG12 15 E2
Holton Heath. RG12 15 H5
Hombrook Dri. RG42 14 A2
Honeyhill Rd. RG12 14 C2
Hopewood Rd. RG12 16 D2
Horatio Av. RG42 15 G2
Hornsby Av. RG12 16 F3
Horsneile La. RG42 14 D1
Hubberholme. RG12 14 C5
Hythe Clo. RG12 15 G6
Illingworth Gro. RG12 15 H2

INDUSTRIAL & RETAIL:
Amen Corner
Business Pk. RG12 14 A3
Arlington Sq
Business Pk. RG12 14 C3
Bilton Ind Est. RG12 14 A5
Eastern Ind Area.
RG12 15 F3
Longshot Ind Est.
RG12 14 A4
Southern Ind Area.
RG12 14 A4
The Arena
Business Pk.RG12 14 C3
The Bracknell Business
Centre. RG12 14 B3
The Peel Centre.
RG12 14 B5
Waterside Pk. RG12 14 A3
Western Ind Area.
RG12 14 B3
Inchwood. RG12 16 E3
Ingleton. RG12 14 C4
Innings La. RG12 15 F2
Iveagh Ct. RG12 15 E6
Jacksons Clo. RG12 16 D1
Jameston. RG12 16 E3
Jevington. RG12 16 E3
Jig's La Sth. RG42 15 F2
Jocks La. RG42 14 A2
Juliet Gdns. RG42 15 G2
Julius Hill. RG42 15 G2
Juniper. RG12 16 E4
Keates Grn. RG42 14 D2
Keepers Coombe. RG12 16 F2
Keldholme. RG12 14 C4
Kenilworth Av. RG12 15 E2
Kennel La. RG42 14 C1
Kenton Clo. RG12 15 E3
Kibble Grn. RG12 16 E1

Kiln La. RG12 14 C3
Kimberley. RG12 16 E3
Kingsmere Rd. RG42 14 B2
Knightswood. RG12 16 D4
Kyle Clo. RG12 14 C4
Ladybank. RG12 16 A2
Lakeside. RG42 15 E1
Lambourne Gro. RG12 15 G3
Lammas Mead. RG42 14 A1
Larges Bridge Dri. RG12 15 E3
Larges La. RG12 15 E3
Latimer. RG12 16 D3
Lauradale. RG12 14 C5
Leafield Copse. RG12 15 H5
Leaves Grn. RG12 16 F2
Leicester. RG12 16 F2
Lemington Gro. RG12 16 D1
Leppington. RG12 16 D3
Letcombe Sq. RG12 15 G5
Leverkusen Rd. RG12 14 D4
Lichfields. RG12 15 G3
Lightwood. RG12 16 F2
Lily Hill Dri. RG12 15 G3
Lily Hill Rd. RG12 15 G3
Lime Walk. RG12 15 E5
Limerick Clo. RG42 14 C2
Linden Hill Rd. RG42 14 B2
Lingwood. RG12 16 E2
Liscombe. RG12 16 E3
Little Ringdale. RG12 15 G5
Littledale Clo. RG12 15 F4
Lochinver. RG12 16 D3
London Rd. RG12 15 E3
Long Hill Rd. RG12 15 H4
Longmoors. RG42 14 A2
Longshot La. RG12 14 A3
Longwater Rd. RG12 16 E2
Lovelace Rd. RG12 14 A5
Lowbury. RG12 15 G5
Ludlow. RG12 16 E3
Lutterworth Clo. RG42 15 E1
Lydbury. RG12 15 G4
Lydney. RG12 16 D3
Lyndhurst Clo. RG12 15 H4
Lynwood Chase. RG12 15 E2
Lytchett Minster Clo.
RG12 15 G6
Lytham. RG12 16 A2
Macbeth Ct. RG42 15 G2
Madingley. RG12 16 D4
Mainprize Rd. RG12 15 E3
Makepiece Rd. RG12 14 D1
Malham Fell. RG12 14 C5
Manor Clo. RG12 14 C1
Mansfield Cres. RG12 16 D1
Manston Dri. RG12 16 D2
Marcheria Clo. RG12 16 D1
Market St. RG12 14 D3
Martins La. RG12 15 F4
Matthews Chase. RG42 14 D1
Meadow Way. RG42 14 B1
Melrose. RG12 16 E3
Membury Walk. RG12 15 G5
Mendip Rd. RG12 15 G6
Merlewood. RG12 15 E6
Merryhill Rd. RG42 14 C1
Micheldever Way.
RG12 15 G6
Milbanke Ct. RG12 14 B3
Milbanke Way. RG12 14 B3
Mill Grn. RG42 14 B3
Mill La. RG12 14 B5
Milman Clo. RG12 15 H3
Milton Clo. RG12 16 D2
Minstead Clo. RG12 15 H4
Moordale Av. RG42 14 A2
Morden Clo. RG12 15 G5
Mount La. RG12 15 E3
Mount Pleasant. RG12 15 E4
Munday Ct. RG12 14 A1
Naseby. RG12 16 D1
Nelson Clo. RG12 15 H3
Netherton. RG12 14 C5
Nettlecombe. RG12 16 F1
New Forest Ride. RG12 15 H6
New Rd. RG12 15 F3
Nightingale Cres. RG12 15 E6
Nine Mile Ride. RG12 16 A4
Norman Keep. RG12 15 H2
Norfolk Chase. RG12 15 H1
North Grn. RG12 15 E3
Northampton Clo. RG12 15 F4
Northcott. RG12 14 C4
Northumberland Clo.
RG42 15 G1

Nuthurst. RG12 15 F6
Nutley. RG12 16 C4
Oak Tree Ms. RG12 15 F4
Oakdale. RG12 16 F2
Oakengates. RG12 16 C4
Oakwood Rd. RG12 15 G3
Oareborough. RG12 15 F5
Octavia. RG12 16 C4
Old Bracknell Clo. RG 14 C4
Old Bracknell La E.
RG12 14 C4
Old Bracknell La W.
RG12 14 D4
Old Farm Dri. RG12 15 E1
Old Lands Hill. RG12 15 E2
Oldbury. RG12 14 B4
Oldstead. RG12 16 F1
Ollerton. RG12 16 C3
Opladen Way. RG12 16 F2
Orion. RG12 16 F2
Ormathwaites Cnr.
RG42 15 G1
Oswald Clo. RG42 15 F1
Othello Gro. RG42 15 G2
Oxenhope. RG12 14 C5
Pakenham Rd. RG12 16 F3
Pankhurst Dri. RG12 15 F6
Park La. RG42 14 A1
Park Rd. RG12 15 G2
Parkland Dri. RG12 15 G2
Patrick Gdns. RG42 15 F1
Peacock La. RG12 14 A4
Pembroke. RG12 16 C3
Pendine Pl. RG12 14 C6
Pendlebury. RG12 16 C3
Penwood Gdns. RG12 16 A2
Peregrine Clo. RG12 14 D6
Perry Oaks. RG12 15 G3
Perry Way. RG12 15 G3
Pewsey Vale. RG12 15 G6
Phillip Clo. RG12 16 F3
Pickering. RG12 14 C5
Picket Post Clo. RG12 15 H4
Plantaganet Pk. RG42 15 H2
Ploughland. RG42 14 B2
Pollardrow Av. RG42 14 B2
Pond Moor Rd. RG12 14 D6
Popham Clo. RG12 15 G6
Portia Gro. RG42 15 G2
Portman Clo. RG12 14 C2
Poyle Gdns. RG12 15 E2
Prescott. RG12 16 B3
Priestwood Av. RG42 14 B2
Priestwood Ct Rd. RG42 14 B2
Primrose Walk. RG12 15 E6
Princess Sq. RG12 14 D3
Priory La. RG42 15 E1
Priory Walk. RG12 15 G5
Quadrant Ct. RG12 15 F4
Qualitas. RG12 16 B4
Quintilis. RG12 16 B4
Rachaels Lake View.
RG12 15 G1
Radcliffe Way. RG12 14 A2
Radnor Rd. RG12 16 C4
Ralph's Ride. RG12 15 F4
Ramsbury Clo. RG12 16 A2
Ramslade Rd. RG12 15 E5
Ranelagh Dri. RG12 15 E4
Rapley Grn. RG12 16 E2
Rectory Clo. RG12 14 D5
Rectory Row. RG12 14 D5
Redditch. RG12 16 F2
Redvers Rd. RG12 14 D6
Reeds Hill. RG12 16 D1
Rickman Clo. RG12 16 E1
Ringmead. RG12 16 A1
Ringwood. RG12 16 B3
Ripplesmere. RG12 15 F5
Roby Dri. RG12 16 F3
Rokeby Clo. RG12 15 E2
Roman Way. RG42 15 H2
Romeo Hill. RG42 15 G2
Rosebank. RG42 14 D1
Rosedale Gdns. RG12 14 C6
Rosset Clo. RG12 14 C5
Rowley Clo. RG12 15 F4
Russell Clo. RG12 15 F3
Rye Clo. RG12 15 E2
Sabin Gates. RG12 14 D4
Saffron Rd. RG12 14 D2
Sage Walk. RG42 15 F1
St Andrews. RG12 16 A2

St Anthonys Clo. RG42 14 C2
Saltire Gdns. RG42 14 C2
Salwey Clo. RG12 16 D2
Samian Pl. RG42 14 A1
Sandford Down. RG12 15 H6
Sandy La. RG12 14 D2
Sarum. RG12 16 A4
Savernake Way. RG12 15 G6
Saxon Dri. RG12 15 H2
Scott Ter. RG12 15 G2
Segsbury Gro. RG12 15 H1
Setley Way. RG12 15 H4
Shaftesbury Clo. RG12 15 E6
Shakespeare Way. RG42 15 G1
Shelley Av. RG12 15 G1
Shepherds Hill. RG12 15 E2
Shepherds La. RG42 14 C1
Sherring Clo. RG42 15 E1
Sherwood Clo. RG12 15 H3
Shropshire Gdns. RG42 15 H1
Silwood. RG12 16 A3
Simmonds Clo. RG42 14 A2
Skelton Fields. RG42 14 D1
Skimped Hill La. RG12 14 C3
Smith Sq. RG12 15 F3
Somerset Gro. RG42 15 H1
South Hill Rd. RG12 16 C2
South Lynn Cres. RG12 14 D6
South Rd. RG12 16 A3
Southwold. RG12 16 A3
Spencer Rd. RG42 14 B2
Spinis. RG12 16 A3
Spinner Grn. RG12 14 C6
Spring Meadow. RG12 15 F2
Stanley Walk. RG12 14 D3
Staplehurst. RG12 16 A3
Statham Ct. RG42 14 A2
Station Rd. RG12 14 D3
Station Way. RG12 14 D3
Staverton Clo. RG12 14 D1
Stokeford Clo. RG12 15 H6
Stoney Rd. RG42 14 B2
Stratfield. RG12 16 A4
Suffolk Combe. RG42 15 H1
Surrey Ct. RG42 15 H1
Swaledale. RG12 16 C1
Swancote Grn. RG12 14 D6
Sweetwell Rd. RG12 14 A3
Swithin Chase. RG42 15 F1
Sycamore Rise. RG12 15 H3
Sylvanus. RG12 16 B3
Sylverns Ct. RG42 15 F1
Tamworth. RG12 16 F3
Target Hill. RG42 15 F1
Tarrant Grn. RG42 15 E1
Tawfield. RG12 16 A3
Tebbit Clo. RG12 15 E3
Temple Way. RG42 14 A1
The Avenue. RG12 14 A4
The Cardinals. RG12 14 D5
The Close. RG12 15 E5
The Crescent. RG12 15 E5
The Croft. RG42 14 D1
The Green. RG12 14 D5
The Oaks. RG12 15 E3
The Paddock. RG12 15 E4
The Ridgeway. RG42 14 D4
The Ring. RG42 14 D3
Thomas Dri. RG42 15 F1
Thornhill. RG12 15 F5
Threshfield. RG12 16 C1
Tidwells Lea. RG42 15 F2
Timline Grn. RG12 15 H3
Toll Gdns. RG12 15 G4
Top Common. RG42 15 E1
Town Centre By-Pass. RG42
Townsend Clo. RG12 15 G6
Trevelyan. RG12 16 A3
Trindle Down. RG42 14 C1
Trumbull Rd. RG42 14 C1
Turnberry. RG12 16 A2
Turnpike Rd. RG12 14 A2
Tytherton. RG12 15 E3
Uffington Dri. RG12 15 G5
Ullswater. RG12 16 A2
Underwood. RG12 16 A2
Upavon Gdns. RG12 15 G6
Upshire Gdns. RG12 15 G5
Vandyke. RG12 16 A2
Viking. RG12 16 A1
Vincent Rise. RG12 15 F4
Viola Croft. RG42 15 G2
Wagbullock Rise. RG12 16 E2

Walbury. RG12 15 G5
Waldron Hill. RG12 15 G2
Wallcroft Clo. RG42 14 A1
Wallingford Clo. RG12 15 G5
Walsh Av. RG42 15 H6
Wantage Clo. RG12 15 F6
Wareham Rd. RG12 15 H6
Warfield Park Farm Dri. RG42
Warfield Rd. RG42 15 E2
Warren Down. RG42 14 A2
Waterham Rd. RG12 16 D2
Wayland Clo. RG12 15 G5
Weather Way. RG12 15 E3
Webb Clo. RG42 14 A1
Welbeck. RG12 16 A1
Wellington Dri. RG12 15 F6
West Gdn. RG12 15 F3
Westcotts Grn. RG42 15 F1
Westcombe Clo. RG12 15 F3
Westbrook Gdns. RG12 15 E2
Western Rd. RG42 14 A2
Westmorland Dri. RG42 15 G1
Westwates Clo. RG12 15 F2
Weycrofts. RG42 14 B1
Whatley Grn. RG12 16 D2
Wheatley. RG12 16 A1
Whistley Clo. RG12 15 F4
Whitton Rd. RG12 15 G4
Wickham Vale. RG12 16 A2
Wilberforce Way. RG12 15 E6
Wilders Clo. RG12 14 C1
Wildridings Rd. RG12 14 B6
Wildridings Sq. RG12 14 C5
Willoughby Rd. RG12 14 B4
Willow Dri. RG12 15 E2
Wilstrode Av. RG42 14 A1
Wilwood Rd. RG42 14 A2
Winchgrove Rd. RG42 14 C1
Windlebrook Grn. RG42 14 C2
Windlesham Rd. RG42 14 B2
Windmill Rd. RG42 14 B2
Windsor Ride. RG12 15 H6
Winscombe. RG12 16 A1
Wittenham Rd. RG12 15 H2
Wokingham Rd. RG42 14 A2
Woodenhill. RG12 16 A4
Woodford Grn. RG12 15 G5
Woodhouse St. RG42 14 A2
Woodland Cres. RG42 15 E1
Woodmere. RG12 15 F5
Woodridge Clo. RG12 14 D4
Woolhampton Way. RG12 15 F6
Worcestershire Lea. RG42 15 H1
Wordsworth. RG12 16 A1
Wroxham. RG12 16 B1
Wychwood Av. RG12 15 H5
Wylam. RG12 16 A1
Wyvern Clo. RG12 14 C5
Yardley. RG12 16 B1
Yorkshire Pl. RG42 15 G1

BRAY

Beaufort Pl. SL6 17 C2
Bray Clo. SL6 17 B2
Bray Rd. SL6 17 A1
Braybank. SL6 17 C2
Brayfield Rd. SL6 17 B2
Church Dri. SL6 17 B2
Church La. SL6 17 B2
Hanover Mead. SL6 17 B2
Hibbert Rd. SL6 17 A1
High St. SL6 17 B2
Monkey Island La. SL6 17 D3
Old Mill La. SL6 17 C2
River Gdns. SL6 17 C2
The Causeway. SL6 17 A2
The Terrace. SL6 17 B2
Upper Bray Rd. SL6 17 B2
Vicarage Dri. SL6 17 A1
Vicarage Walk. SL6 17 A1

BURGHFIELD COMMON

Abbey Park. RG7 17 A4
Abbots Rd. RG7 17 A5
Alder Glade. RG7 17 A4
Alison Clo. RG7 17 B6
Anstey Pl. RG7 17 C4
Ash La. RG7 17 B4
Auclum Clo. RG7 17 C5
Auclum La. RG7 17 C5
Badgers Glade RG7 17 B5
Bannister Rd. RG7 17 A5
Barn Owl Way. RG7 17 C4
Birch Rd. RG7 17 B4
Blackbird Clo. RG7 17 C4
Blands Clo. RG7 17 A5
Bluebell Dri. RG7 17 A4
Boldrewood. RG7 17 B5
Bracken Way. RG7 17 B6
Brocas Rd. RG7 17 A6
Bunces La. RG7 17 B6
Burdock Clo. RG7 17 C5
Chervil Way. RG7 17 C5
Clayhill Rd. RG7 17 A4
Coltsfoot Clo. RG7 17 C4
Dauntless Rd. RG7 17 C4
Field Clo. RG7 17 C5
Finch Way. RG7 17 C4
Firs End. RG7 17 B5
Fox Clo. RG7 17 B5
Garlands Clo. RG7 17 B6
Goodwood Clo. RG7 17 B5
Goring La. RG7 17 B6
Granby End. RG7 17 C4
Great Auclum Pl. RG7 17 C5
Hannigtons Way. RG7 17 D4
Hawksworth Rd. RG7 17 C4
Headlands Ct. RG7 17 A6
Hermits Clo. RG7 17 C5
Highfield Ct. RG7 17 C4
Hillside. RG7 17 D4
Hollybush La. RG7 17 A4
Holmdene. RG7 17 C4
Hornbeam Pightle. RG7 17 C4
Horseshoe Cres. RG7 17 C4
Hunters Hill. RG7 17 B4
Jordans La. RG7 17 A5
Kennet Pl. RG7 17 C5
Kestrel Way. RG7 17 C4
Kirkwood Cres. RG7 17 A4
Lamden Way. RG7 17 C4
Lockram Rd. RG7 17 C6
Loves Clo. RG7 17 B4
Mans Hill. RG7 17 D4
Myrtle Clo. RG7 17 C4
Normoor Rd. RG7 17 A6
Oak Dri. RG7 17 B5
Oakdene. RG7 17 A6
Omers Rise. RG7 17 A4
Padworth Rd. RG7 17 B6
Palmers La. RG7 17 B6
Pembroke Clo. RG7 17 D4
Pinchcut. RG7 17 B4
Pine Ridge Rd. RG7 17 B4
Ragdale. RG7 17 C4
Reading Rd. RG7 17 B6
Recreation Rd. RG7 17 B5
Robin Clo. RG7 17 C4
Russet Glade. RG7 17 C5
St Marys Way. RG7 17 C4
Saxby Clo. RG7 17 C4
School La. RG7 17 B5
Sorrel Clo. RG7 17 C4
Southwood Gdns. RG7 17 B4
Spring Wood La. RG7 17 B5
Stable Clo. RG7 17 B4
Sun Gdns. RG7 17 B6
Tanners Clo. RG7 17 B6
Tarragon Way. RG7 17 C5
The Close. RG7 17 B6
Three Firs Way. RG7 17 A6
Thrush Clo. RG7 17 C4
Totterdown. RG7 17 A6
Valley Rd. RG7 17 B4
Warren Clo. RG7 17 B5
Wheeler Clo. RG7 17 B5
Woodlands Av. RG7 17 B4
Woodmans La. RG7 17 A5
Wren Clo. RG7 17 C4

COOKHAM

Abney Court Dri. SL8 19 H1
Alleyns La. SL6 18 D3
Andrews Reach. SL8 19 H1
Barnfield Clo. SL6 19 F6
Bass Mead. SL6 19 F6
Bedwins La. SL6 18 B5
Berries Rd. SL6 19 H4
Bigfirth La SL6 18 B5
Black Butts Cotts. SL6 19 H4
Bradcutts La. SL6 19 C2
Briar Glen. SL6 19 E5
Bridge Av. SL6 19 F5
Broom Hill. SL6 19 E5
Burnt Oak. SL6 19 H4
Cannondown Rd. SL6 19 E6
Causeway. SL6 19 G4
Cedar Dri. SL6 19 G4
Choke La. SL6 18 B6
Church Rd. SL6 18 B5
Cookham
Dean Bottom. SL6 18 C3
Coombe End. SL6 18 B5
Coxborrow Clo. SL6 19 F4
Danes Gdns. SL6 19 F5
Deans La. SL6 18 C3
Dedmere Rd. SL7 18 A1
East Paddock. SL6 18 A5
Elizabeth Clo. SL6 19 F4
Ferry La. SL8 19 H2
Fieldhouse La. SL7 18 A1
Fieldhouse Way. SL7 18 A1
First Av. SL7 18 A1
Firview Clo. SL7 18 A2
Fourth Av. SL7 18 A1
Gainsborough. SL6 19 F5
Gibralter La. SL6 18 C2
Gorse Rd. SL6 19 E5
Gossmore Clo. SL7 18 A2
Gossmore Wk. SL7 18 A2
Graham Rd. SL6 19 E5
Grange La. SL6 19 F3
Grange Rd. SL6 19 F4
Groves Way. SL6 19 F5
Grubwood La. SL6 18 B5
Halldore Rd. SL6 19 E4
Hardings Grn. SL6 18 C4
Hedsor Rd. SL6 19 H1
High Rd. SL6 19 H4
High St. SL6 19 H4
Hillcrest Av. SL6 19 E5
Hills La. SL6 18 D4
Hockett La. SL6 18 A5
Hollybush La. SL6 18 B5
Hyde Grn. SL7S 18 A2

INDUSTRIAL & RETAIL:
Globe Park. SL7 18 A1
Wessex La
Ind Pk. SL8 19 H1

Inwood Clo. SL6 18 B5
Jeffries Ct. SL8 19 G1
Jobs La. SL6 18 C3
Kennel La. SL6 18 C4
Kings La. SL6 18 C3
Lesters Rd. SL6 19 E5
Lightlands La. SL6 19 F6
Long La. SL6 18 C6
Lower Rd. SL6 19 E4
Lyndhurst Av. SL6 19 E5
Maidenhead Rd. SL6 19 F5
Marlow By-Pass. SL7 18 A3
Meadow Clo. SL7 18 A2
Mill La. SL6 19 H4
New Rd. SL6 19 E4
Newfield Gdns. SL7 18 A1
Odney La. SL6 19 H4
Orchard Hill. SL6 19 H2
Parkway. SL7 18 A1
Peace La. SL6 19 F5
Pearce Dri. SL6 19 F4
Penling Clo. SL6 19 E5
Popes La. SL6 18 C3
Poundfield La. SL6 19 F4
Quarry Wood Rd. SL7 18 A3
Quarrydale Dri. SL7 18 A1
River Park Dri. SL7 18 A2
Riverdale. SL8 19 H3
Riverwood Av. SL7 18 B2
Riverwood Dri. SL7 18 A2
Roman Lea. SL6 19 F4
Rose Bank Clo. SL6 19 E4
Savill Way. SL7 18 A1
School La,
Cookham. SL6 19 H4
School La,
Cookham Dean. SL6 18 C4
Shergold Way. SL6 19 F5
Southwood Gdns. SL6 19 E6
Southwood Rd. SL6 19 E6
Spencers La. SL6 19 E4
Spring La. SL6 18 C6
Startins La. SL6 18 C3
Station Hill. SL6 19 F4
Station Rd. SL6 19 F4
Stone House La. SL6 18 D2
Strand La. SL6 19 F6
Strand View Wk. SL6 19 F6
Stubbles La. SL6 18 B5
Sutton Clo. SL6 19 H4
Sutton Rd. SL6 19 H4
Switchback Rd Nth. SL6 19 E6
Terrys La. SL6 19 E2
The Acre. SL7 18 A1
The Pound. SL6 19 G4
The Shaw. SL6 19 E5
Third Av. SL7 18 A1
Vicarage Clo. SL6 19 H4
Vivian Clo. SL6S 19 F5
Wakelins End. SL6 19 H4
Walnut Tree Clo. SL8 19 H1
Walnut Way. SL8 19 H1
Warners Hill. SL6 18 D4
Wessons Hill. SL6 18 C4
Wessex Rd. SL8 19 F5
Westwood Grn. SL6 19 F5
Whiteladyes La. SL6 19 E4
Windmill Rd. SL6 19 E5
Winter Hill. SL6 18 B3
Winter Hill Rd. SL6 18 A5
Woodmoor End. SL6 19 E4
Worster Rd. SL6 19 E5

CROWTHORNE

Addiscombe Rd. RG45 21 G5
Albert Rd. RG45 21 F4
Albert Wk. RG45 21 G4
Alcot Clo. RG45 21 F5
Alderbrook Clo. RG45 20 D6
Aldworth Gdns. RG45 21 E3
Ardwell Clo. RG45 20 D4
Arenal Dri. RG45 21 G6
Ashdale Pk. RG40 20 B3
Badgers Set. RG45 21 E4
Barracane Dri. RG45 21 F4
Barwell Clo. RG45 20 D5
Belmont Rd. RG45 21 F3
Benbridge Ct. RG45 20 D4
Benson Rd. RG45 20 D4
Birch Side. RG45 21 E3
Blake Clo. RG45 21 G5
Bowman Ct. RG45 20 D5
Bracknell Rd. RG45 21 E4
Bramble Gate. RG45 21 E3
Bramley Ct. RG45 20 C5
Bramley Gro. RG45 20 C3
Brookers Corner. RG45 21 G4
Brookers Row. RG45 21 G3
Brunel Dri. RG45 21 G1
Butler Rd. RG45 21 F3
Byron Dri. RG45 21 F6
Cambridge Rd. RG45 21 G5
Carnation Clo. RG45 21 E1
Celandine Clo. RG45 21 H5
Chaplains Hill. RG45 21 H5
Chaucer Rd. RG45 21 F4
Church Rd East. RG45 21 F4
Church Rd West. RG45 21 F5
Church St. RG45 21 F5
Circle Hill Rd. RG45 21 G4
Club La. RG45 21 H4
Coleridge Clo. RG45 21 G5
Connaught Clo. RG45 20 D5
Copenhagen Wk. RG45 21 F5
Coppice Gdns. RG45 21 E4
Corsham Way. RG45 21 E4
Cricket Field Gro. RG45 21 H4
Dormer Clo. RG45 21 E4
Dowding Ct. RG45 21 G3
Duchess Clo. RG45 21 F2
Dukes Ride. RG45 20 C5
Dukes Wood. RG45 21 F4
Eagle Clo. RG45 21 E3
Edgcumbe Park Dri. RG45 21 E4
Edgdale Clo. RG45 21 F5
Edgewood Clo. RG45 21 F3
Elgar Av. RG45 21 F3
Ellis Rd. RG45 21 F3
Everest Rd. RG45 21 F3
Farm Clo. RG45 21 G2
Fern Clo. RG45 21 G2
Ferry Clo. RG45 21 E2
Fielding Gdns. RG45 21 F5

Fincham End Dri. RG45 20 D5
Forest Rd. RG45 21 G4
Fosse Way. RG45 21 E4
Frensham Rd. RG45 21 F3
Furzehill Cres. RG45 21 G5
Geranium Clo. RG45 21 E1
Goldsmith Way. RG45 21 F5
Gordon Rd. RG45 21 H6
Grange Av. RG45 21 F3
Grant Rd. RG45 21 G6
Greenfield Way. RG45 21 E2
Greenfinch Clo. RG45 21 E3
Greenside. RG45 21 E4
Greenwood Rd. RG45 21 E3
Greystoke Ct. RG45 21 F5
Grove Clo. RG40 20 C2
Hardy Grn. RG45 21 F5
Hatch Ride. RG45 21 E1
Heath Hill Rd Nth. RG45 21 F4
Heath Hill Rd Sth. RG45 21 F4
Heath Ride. RG40 20 A3
Heather Way. RG45 21 F4
Heatherdene Av. RG45 20 C5
Heathermount Dri.
 RG45 21 E3
Heathermount Gdns.
 RG45 21 E3
Heathlands Rd. RG40 20 D1
High St. RG45 21 G5
Highway. RG45 21 E4
Hillary Dri. RG45 21 F3
Hinton Clo. RG45 21 F2
Hinton Dri. RG45 21 F2
Hollybush Ride. RG45 20 A5
Hollyhook Clo. RG45 21 E3
Holmbury Av. RG45 21 E2
Holme Clo. RG45 21 E2
Honey Hill. RG40 21 E1
Honeysuckle Clo. RG45 21 E2
Houston Way. RG45 20 C4
INDUSTRIAL & RETAIL:
The Crowthorne
 Business Est. RG45 21 G2
Wellington
 Business Pk. RG45 20 D5
Jerome Cnr. RG45 21 G6
Keats Way. RG45 21 F3
Kentigern Dri. RG45 21 H4
Kings Rd. RG45 21 G5
Kingsbridge Cotts.
 RG40 20 C2
Kingsley Clo. RG45 21 F6
Knowles Av. RG45 20 D4
Lake End Way. RG45 21 F5
Larkswood Dri. RG45 21 G4
Leacroft. RG45 21 F4
Leith Clo. RG45 21 F2
Leyside. RG45 21 F4
Linkway. RG45 21 G5
Little Fryth. RG40 20 B3
Llangar Gro. RG45 21 E4
Lower Broadmoor Rd.
 RG45 21 G5
Lower Wokingham Rd.
 RG40 20 B2
Lupin Ride. RG45 21 F1
Lyneham Rd. RG45 21 F4
Lyon Rd. RG45 21 G2
Macadam Av. RG45 21 G2
Maple Dri. RG45 21 G2
Marigold Clo. RG45 21 E2
Masefield Gdns. RG45 21 F6
Merryman Dri. RG45 21 E3
Mordaunt Dri. RG45 21 F6
Mulberry Clo. RG45 21 G5
Napier Clo. RG45 21 G5
Napier Rd. RG45 21 G5
New Rd. RG45 21 G4
New Wokingham Rd.
 RG45 21 E2
Nine Mile Ride. RG40 20 B2
Nine Mile Ride. RG45 21 E1
Nugee Ct. RG45 21 G4
Oaklands La. RG45 21 E3
Old Pharmacy Ct.
 RG45 21 G5
Old Sawmill La. RG45 21 G3
Old Wokingham Rd,
 Crowthorne. RG45 21 G1
Old Wokingham Rd,
 Wokingham. RG40 21 G1
Oleander Clo. RG45 21 E2
Otter Clo. RG45 21 E2
Palmer Clo. RG40 21 E1

Parkway. RG45 21 E4
Pensford Clo. RG45 21 F2
Pinefields Clo. RG45 21 F5
Pinehill Rd. RG45 21 G5
Pinewood Av. RG45 21 G3
Polyanthus Way. RG45 21 F2
Priors Wood. RG45 20 C5
Purcell Rd. RG45 21 F2
Queens Ride. RG45 21 F1
Range Rd. RG40 20 A2
Ravenswood Av. RG45 20 D5
Roman Ride. RG45 20 B4
Rowan Dri. RG45 21 G2
Royal Oak Dri. RG45 21 F1
Ruskin Ct. RG45 20 D5
St Andrews Clo. RG45 20 D3
St Johns St. RG45 21 F4
St Sebastians Clo.
 RG40 20 D1
Salamanca. RG45 20 C4
Sandhurst Rd. RG45 20 A1
Sandhurst Rd. RG45 21 F6
School Rd. RG45 21 H5
Seymour Ct. RG45 20 C5
Shaw Pk. RG45 20 C5
Shepherds Way. RG45 20 C5
Soldiers Rise. RG40 20 B2
South Meadow. RG45 21 H6
Squirrels Drey. RG45 21 E4
Sweetbriar. RG45 21 E2
Sydney Clo. RG45 21 G2
Talisman Clo. RG45 20 C4
Telford Av. RG45 21 G2
The Avenue. RG45 21 F3
The Bracken. RG45 21 E2
The Brambles. RG45 20 C3
The Chase. RG45 21 E3
The Conifers. RG45 21 E2
The Devils Highway.
 RG45 20 D4
The Paddock. RG45 21 E3
The Rise. RG45 21 E4
The Terrace. RG45 21 H4
Thornbury Clo. RG45 21 F4
Thorne Clo. RG45 21 E2
Timberley Pl. RG45 20 C4
Towers Dri. RG45 21 F5
Upper Broadmoor Rd.
 RG45 21 G4
Walmer Clo. RG45 21 G4
Waterloo Rd. RG45 21 E5
Wellesley Dri. RG45 20 C4
Wellington Rd. RG45 21 G5
Wellingtonia Av. RG45 20 A5
Wentworth Clo. RG45 21 E2
Westbury Clo. RG45 21 F4
White City. RG45 21 H4
Wiltshire Av. RG45 21 F3
Wokingham Rd. RG45 20 C5
Wood End. RG45 20 D5

DATCHET
Adelaide Rd. SL4 22 A3
Beaulieu Rd. SL3 22 B3
Buccleuch Rd. SL3 22 B2
Cobb Clo. SL3 22 D3
Datchet Pl. SL3 22 C3
Deep Field. SL3 22 C2
Ditton Rd. SL3 22 D3
Dutch Elm Av. SL4 22 A2
Elmcroft. SL3 22 C3
Eton Clo. SL3 22 A1
Eton Rd. SL3 22 A1
Fairfield Av. SL3 22 C2
Fairfield Clo. SL3 22 D2
Gables Clo. SL3 22 A1
Green La. SL3 22 C3
Hall Ct. SL3 22 B2
High St. SL3 22 B2
Holmlea Rd. SL3 22 D3
Holmlea Walk. SL3 22 C3
Horton Rd. SL3 22 B2
Lawn Clo. SL3 22 C2
Leigh Pk. SL3 22 C2
Lime Av. SL3 22 A2
Linchfield Rd. SL3 22 C2
Link Rd. SL3 22 C2
London Rd. SL3 22 A1
Majors Farm Rd. SL3 22 D2
Manor House La. SL3 22 B2
Marshfield. SL3 22 C3

Mill Pl. SL3 22 D3
Montagu Rd. SL3 22 B3
Montrose Av. SL3 22 C2
Montrose Way. SL3 22 D2
New Rd. SL3 22 D3
Penn Rd. SL3 22 D3
Percy Pl. SL3 22 C2
Prince Alberts Wk. SL4 22 A2
Priory Way. SL3 22 B2
Queen Victorias Wk
 SL4 22 A3
Queens Mead. SL3 22 B2
Queens Rd. SL4 22 B2
Riding Court Rd. SL3 22 C2
Ruscombe Gdns. SL3 22 B1
Saffron Clo. SL3 22 C3
Slough Rd. SL3 22 B1
Southlea Rd. SL3 22 B3
Talbot Pl. SL3 22 D3
The Avenue. SL3 22 B3
The Drive. SL3 22 C3
The Green. SL3 22 B2
The Paddock. SL3 22 B3
Whites La. SL3 22 B1
Windsor Rd. SL3 22 A1

HUNGERFORD
Aldbourne Clo. RG17 23 C3
Atherton Cres. RG17 23 B4
Atherton Rd. RG17 23 B4
Bearwater. RG17 23 C1
Bourne Vale. RG17 23 A4
Breach Sq. RG17 23 C5
Bridge St. RG17 23 C2
Bulpit La. RG17 23 C5
Canal Walk. RG17 23 C2
Chantry Mead. RG17 23 A4
Chapel Ct. RG17 23 C1
Charnham La. RG17 23 C1
Charnham Park. RG17 23 B1
Charnham St. RG17 23 B1
Cherry Gro. RG17 23 B3
Chestnut Walk. RG17 23 C5
Chilton Way. RG17 23 B3
Church Croft. RG17 23 B2
Church La. RG17 23 C2
Church St. RG17 23 B3
Church Way. RG17 23 B3
Clarks Gdns. RG17 23 C4
Coldharbour Rd. RG17 23 C5
Coombe Vw. RG17 23 C6
Croft Rd. RG17 23 B3
Crown Mews. RG17 23 C3
Cygnet Way. RG17 23 C1
De Montfort Gro. RG17 23 B5
Eddington Hill. RG17 23 D1
Everland Rd. RG17 23 C2
Fairfields. RG17 23 C4
Fairview Rd. RG17 23 C4
Faulkner Sq. RG17 23 C1
Freemans Clo. RG17 23 A3
Hamblin Mdw. RG17 23 D1
Herongate. RG17 23 B1
High St. RG17 23 C1
Hillside Rd. RG17 23 C5
Homefield Way. RG17 23 B3
Honeyfields. RG17 23 B3
Inkpen Rd. RG17 23 D6
Kennet Ct. RG17 23 D1
Kennet Way. RG17 23 C1
Liguiel Clo. RG17 23 C6
Lancaster Clo. RG17 23 B5
Lancaster Sq. RG17 23 B5
Lewingston Ms. RG17 23 C4
Macklin Clo. RG17 23 C3
Marsh La. RG17 23 A3
Middletons Clo. RG17 23 D1
Moores Pl. RG17 23 C4
Morley Pl. RG17 23 C4
North Vw. RG17 23 B3
Oakes Ct. RG17 23 B3
Orchard Park Clo.
 RG17 23 C4
Oxford St. RG17 23 D1
Park St. RG17 23 C3
Park Way. RG17 23 C3
Parsonage La. RG17 23 C1
Port Down. RG17 23 D3
Pound Piece. RG17 23 A3
Priory Av. RG17 23 C5
Priory Clo. RG17 23 C5

Priory Rd. RG17 23 B4
Priory Ter. RG17 23 C4
Prospect Rd. RG17 23 B4
Ramsbury Dri. RG17 23 D3
Regent Clo. RG17 23 B4
St Lawrence Sq. RG17 23 B3
Salisbury Rd. RG17 23 A6
Sanden Clo. RG17 23 B4
Sarum Way. RG17 23 B4
Shalbourne Clo. RG17 23 A3
Smitham Bridge Rd.
 RG17 23 A3
Somerset Clo. RG17 23 A3
South Vw. RG17 23 C4
Station Rd. RG17 23 C3
Strongrove Hill. RG17 23 A1
Swangate. RG17 23 C1
Tarrants Hill. RG17 23 C4
Tealgate. RG17 23 B1
The Croft. RG17 23 B2
The Forge. RG17 23 C2
Townsview. RG17 23 C3
Uplands. RG17 23 B4
Warum Clo. RG17 23 D1
Wessex Clo. RG17 23 A3
Westbrook Clo. RG17 23 A4
Wiltshire Clo. RG17 23 A3
York Rd. RG17 23 B5

LAMBOURN
Aintree. RG17 22 C5
Atherton Pl. RG17 22 B5
Baydon Rd. RG17 22 A6
Beales Farm Clo. RG17 22 C6
Big La. RG17 22 B5
Blind La. RG17 22 C6
Bockhampton Rd. RG17 22 C6
Chapel La. RG17 22 C5
Child St. RG17 22 B5
Church Clo. RG17 22 B5
Close End. RG17 22 B5
Crowle Rd. RG17 22 B5
Derby Clo. RG17 22 B5
Edwards Hill. RG17 22 B5
Essex Pl. RG17 22 B4
Flintjack Pl. RG17 22 B5
Folly Rd. RG17 22 A5
Foxbury. RG17 22 C4
Francomes Field. RG17 22 C6
Goose Grn. RG17 22 C4
Greenway. RG17 22 B6
Gwyns Piece. RG17 22 C6
Harris Clo. RG17 22 C5
High St. RG17 22 B5
Honey Hill. RG17 22 C4
Hungerford Hill. RG17 22 B6
Lambourn Pl. RG17 22 B5
Lion Mews. RG17 22 C5
Long Hedge. RG17 22 D6
Lynch La. RG17 22 B4
Mill La. RG17 22 C5
Millfield. RG17 22 C5
Montague St. RG17 22 C5
Newbury Rd. RG17 22 C5
Newbury St. RG17 22 C5
North Farm Clo. RG17 22 C4
Northfields. RG17 22 C4
Oxford St. RG17 22 B5
Parsonage Pl. RG17 22 B5
Parsonage Rd. RG17 22 B5
Pegasus Ct. RG17 22 C5
Rockfel Rd. RG17 22 B5
St Agnes Ter. RG17 22 B5
St Michaels Clo. RG17 22 B5
Sheep Fair Way. RG17 22 B6
Sheepdrove Rd. RG17 22 C4
Southbank Gdns. RG17 22 C6
Station Rd. RG17 22 C5
The Classics. RG17 22 C6
The Old School Yd.
 RG17 22 B5
The Old Station Yd.
 RG17 22 C6
The Park. RG17 22 B4
Three Post La. RG17 22 B5
Tubbs Farm Clo. RG17 22 C5
Upper Lambourn Rd.
 RG17 22 A4
Walkers La. RG17 22 C4
Wantage Rd. RG17 22 C5

Woodbury. RG17 22 C6

MAIDENHEAD
Abell Gdns. SL6 24 B2
Addison Ct. SL6 25 H2
Albert St. SL6 25 F5
Aldebury Rd. SL6 25 F1
Aldwick Dri. SL6 24 D5
Alexandra Rd. SL6 24 D3
All Saints Av. SL6 24 D3
Allenby Rd. SL6 24 B4
Alston Gdns. SL6 25 F4
Altwood Bailey. SL6 24 C6
Altwood Clo. SL6 24 B6
Altwood Dri. SL6 24 B6
Altwood Rd. SL6 24 A6
Alwyn Rd. SL6 24 B3
Anne Clo. SL6 25 E1
Archer Clo. SL6 24 D3
Arlington Clo. SL6 24 A3
Arundel Clo. SL6 24 A3
Ashcroft Rd. SL6 24 A3
Ashley Park. SL6 25 H1
Ashton Pl. SL6 24 B5
Astor Clo. SL6 25 H5
Athlone Clo. SL6 25 E2
Auckland Clo. SL6 25 H3
Audley Dri. SL6 24 C5
Austins Gate. SL6 24 A3
Australia Av. SL6 25 F3
Autumn Walk. SL6 24 A5
Avenue Rd. SL6 25 H6
Avondale. SL6 24 C2
Bad Godesberg Way.
 SL6 25 F4
Badminton Rd. SL6 24 C5
Bailey Clo. SL6 25 F4
Bakers La. SL6 24 A3
Balmoral. SL6 24 C2
Bannard Rd. SL6 24 A6
Bargeman Rd. SL6 25 E6
Barn Clo. SL6 25 F1
Bath Ct. SL6 24 D5
Bath Rd. SL6 24 A5
Beech Clo. SL6 24 C3
Beechwood Dri. SL6 24 B5
Bell St. SL6 25 F5
Belmont Cres. SL6 24 D3
Belmont Dri. SL6 24 D2
Belmont Park Av. SL6 24 D2
Belmont Park Rd. SL6 24 D3
Belmont Rd. SL6 24 D3
Belmont Vale. SL6 24 D3
Berkeley Clo. SL6 24 A3
Beverley Gdns. SL6 24 B2
Birdwood Rd. SL6 24 B4
Bishop Ct. SL6 24 D5
Bix La. SL6 24 A2
Blackamore La. SL6 25 G3
Blakeney Ct. SL6 25 F2
Blenheim Rd. SL6 24 B3
Blomfield Rd. SL6 24 B6
Boyn Gro. SL6 24 C5
Boyn Hill Av. SL6 24 D5
Boyn Hill Clo. SL6 24 D6
Boyn Hill Rd. SL6 24 D6
Boyn Valley Rd. SL6 24 D6
Boyndon Rd. SL6 25 E4
Brampton Ct. SL6 25 H3
Bray Rd. SL6 25 H5
Braywick Rd. SL6 25 F5
Briar Dene. SL6 24 C2
Bridge Av. SL6 25 G4
Bridge Rd. SL6 25 G4
Bridge St. SL6 25 G4
Bridle Clo. SL6 25 E2
Bridle Rd. SL6 25 E2
Broadway. SL6 25 F5
Brock La. SL6 25 F4
Brompton Dri. SL6 24 C1
Brookdene Clo. SL6 25 F1
Brunel Clo. SL6 25 E6
Brunel Rd. SL6 25 E6
Calder Clo. SL6 25 E2
Calder Ct. SL6 25 E6
Camden Rd. SL6 24 D2
Camley Gdns. SL6 24 A3
Camley Park Dri. SL6 24 A3
Camperdown. SL6 25 H2
Cannock Clo. SL6 25 H5
Cannon Court Rd. SL6 24 D1

Cannon La. SL6 24 A6
Carisbrook Clo. SL6 24 C5
Castle Ct. SL6 25 E4
Castle Dri. SL6 25 E4
Castle Hill. SL6 25 E4
Castle Hill Ter. SL6 25 E4
Castle Ms. SL6 25 E4
Cedars Rd. SL6 25 G4
Chalgrove Clo. SL6 25 H5
Challow Ct. SL6 25 E2
Chatsworth Clo. SL6 24 C6
Chauntry Rd. SL6 25 H5
Cheniston Grn. SL6 24 A4
Cherington Gate. SL6 24 B2
Cherwell Clo. SL6 25 G3
Chestnut Clo. SL6 25 H2
Cheviot Clo. SL6 25 H5
Chiltern Rd. SL6 25 H5
Church Rd. SL6 25 H6
Clappers Mdw. SL6 25 H2
Clare Rd. SL6 24 D5
Clarefield Clo. SL6 24 B2
Clarefield Dri. SL6 24 B2
Clarefield Rd. SL6 24 C2
Cleveland Clo. SL6 25 H5
Cliveden Mead. SL6 25 H1
Clivemont Rd. SL6 25 F2
College Av. SL6 25 E4
College Glen. SL6 24 D4
College Rise. SL6 24 D4
College Rd. SL6 25 E3
Collier Clo. SL6 25 F2
Coln Clo. SL6 25 F3
Compton Dri. SL6 24 A3
Connaught Clo. SL6 25 E2
Cookham Rd. SL6 25 F1
Cope Ct. SL6 24 C4
Cordwallis Rd. SL6 25 E3
Cordwallis St. SL6 25 E3
Corfe Pl. SL6 24 C4
Cornwall Clo. SL6 25 E1
Cotswold Clo. SL6 25 H5
Courtfield Dri. SL6 24 C5
Courthouse Rd. SL6 24 C4
Courtlands. SL6 25 F5
Cranbrook Dri. SL6 24 B2
Craufurd Rise. SL6 25 E3
Creden Clo. SL6 24 D3
Crescent Dri. SL6 25 E4
Cromwell Rd. SL6 24 D4
Crown La. SL6 25 G4
Croxley Rise. SL6 24 D5
Culham Rd. SL6 25 E1
Deerswood. SL6 25 H2
Denham Clo. SL6 24 C5
Denmark St. SL6 25 F3
Depot Rd. SL6 25 F5
Derwent Dri. SL6 24 D3
Desborough Cres. SL6 24 D6
Dhoon Rise. SL6 25 F5
Donnington Gdns. SL6 25 F2
Dorchester Clo. SL6 24 C2
East Rd. SL6 25 F4
Edinburgh Rd. SL6 25 E2
Edith Rd. SL6 24 B4
Ellington Pk. SL6 25 E2
Elm Gro. SL6 25 E4
Elton Dri. SL6 25 E3
Evenlode. SL6 25 F3
Fair Acre. SL6 24 D5
Fairford Rd. SL6 25 F3
Fane Way. SL6 24 D6
Farm Clo. SL6 24 A4
Farm Rd. SL6 24 A4
Farmers Way. SL6 24 A6
Fawley Ct. SL6 25 E1
Fernley Ct. SL6 25 E2
Fielding Rd. SL6 24 C4
Finch Ct. SL6 24 D6
Florence Av. SL6 25 G3
Fontwell Clo. SL6 24 A3
Forlease Ct. SL6 25 G5
Forlease Dri. SL6 25 G5
Forlease Rd. SL6 25 G4
Fotherby Ct. SL6 25 G5
Frascati Way. SL6 25 F4
Fullbrook Clo. SL6 25 G3
Fullers Yd. SL6 25 H1
Furze Platt Rd. SL6 24 A1
Furze Rd. SL6 25 E2
Gables Clo. SL6 25 H3
Gardner Rd. SL6 25 E1
Garthlands. SL6 24 D1
Glebe Rd. SL6 25 H6
Gloucester Rd. SL6 25 E1
Gordon Rd. SL6 24 D4
Grafton Clo. SL6 25 E1
Graham Clo. SL6 24 C6
Grassy La. SL6 25 E4
Grays Alley. SL6 24 A4
Great Hill Cres. SL6 24 C6
Green Clo. SL6 25 F2
Green La. SL6 25 G5
Greenfields. SL6 25 G5
Greenways Dri. SL6 24 B3
Grenfell Av. SL6 25 F5
Grenfell Pl. SL6 25 F5
Grenfell Rd. SL6 25 E4
Griffin Clo. SL6 25 E6
Gringer Hill. SL6 25 E2
Grove Rd. SL6 25 G4
Gwendale. SL6 24 C2
Haddon Rd. SL6 24 C6
Halifax Clo. SL6 24 B3
Halifax Rd. SL6 24 B3
Halifax Way. SL6 24 B3
Hamilton Pk. SL6 24 B5
Hampden Rd. SL6 24 B3
Hardwick Clo. SL6 24 A3
Hare Shots. SL6 25 E6
Harefield Rd. SL6 24 B4
Hargrave Rd. SL6 25 E3
Harrow Clo. SL6 25 F2
Harrow La. SL6 25 E2
Hatfield Clo. SL6 24 C5
Havelock Cres. SL6 24 C4
Havelock Rd. SL6 24 C4
Hawthorn Gdns. SL6 25 E6
Hazel Clo. SL6 25 G3
Headington Clo. SL6 24 A4
Headington Rd. SL6 24 A3
Heathlands Dri. SL6 24 A5
Hedingham Mews. SL6 24 D4
Helmsdale. SL6 24 C2
Henley Rd. SL6 24 A4
Hever Clo. SL6 24 C5
High St. SL6 25 F4
High Town Rd. SL6 25 E5
Highfield Rd. SL6 24 C3
Highgrove Pk. SL6 25 E3
Highway Av. SL6 24 B4
Highway Rd. SL6 24 B5
Hillside. SL6 25 E6
Hobbis Dri. SL6 24 B5
Holly Dri. SL6 25 F3
Holmanleaze. SL6 25 G3
Holmwood Clo. SL6 24 B6
Homeside Clo. SL6 25 E1
Horseguards Dri. SL6 25 H4
Howarth Rd. SL6 25 G5
Hughendon Clo. SL6 24 C5
Ilchester Clo. SL6 24 D6
INDUSTRIAL & RETAIL:
Cordwallis Pk. SL6 25 E2
Vanwall Business Pk. SL6 24 C6
In The Ray. SL6 25 H3
Juniper Dri. SL6 25 H3
Keble Rd. SL6 25 E3
Kennedy Clo. SL6 24 C5
Kennet Rd. SL6 25 F3
Kent Way. SL6 25 E2
Kenwood Clo. SL6 24 B4
Keys La. SL6 25 F5
Kidwells Clo. SL6 25 F3
King St. SL6 25 F5
Kings Dri. SL6 25 E5
Kings Gro. SL6 25 E5
Kingswood Ct. SL6 25 G6
Knowlsey Clo. SL6 24 B2
Laburnham Rd. SL6 25 E5
Laggan Rd. SL6 25 F2
Laggan Sq. SL6 25 F2
Lake View. SL6 25 G2
Lakeside. SL6 25 H2
Lancaster Rd. SL6 24 B3
Lancastria Mews. SL6 25 E4
Langdale Clo. SL6 25 G5
Langton Clo. SL6 24 D3
Lantern Walk. SL6 25 H4
Larchfield Rd. SL6 25 E6
Lassell Gdns. SL6 25 H4
Lee La. SL6 24 A2
Lees Clo. SL6 24 B6
Lees Gdns. SL6 24 B6
Leighton Gdns. SL6 25 H2
Lexington Av. SL6 24 D6
Lime Walk. SL6 24 A3
Lincoln Rd. SL6 24 B3
Linden Av. SL6 24 D2
Lingholm Clo. SL6 24 D5
Lissett Rd. SL6 25 G5
Loddon Dri. SL6 24 D3
Longleat Gdns. SL6 24 D5
Lonsdale Clo. SL6 25 G2
Lower Boyndon Rd. SL6 25 E5
Ludlow Rd. SL6 25 E5
Lutmans La. SL6 25 F1
Lyneham Gdns. SL6 24 C2
Lynton Grn. SL6 25 E4
Maidenhead Rd. SL6 25 E1
Mallow Pk. SL6 24 C2
Malvern Rd. SL6 25 D2
Maple Clo. SL6 24 D6
Market St. SL6 25 F4
Marlborough Clo. SL6 24 B5
Marlborough Rd. SL6 24 B5
Marlow Rd. SL6 25 F4
Martin Clo. SL6 25 F3
Meadway. SL6 25 G4
Medallion Pl. SL6 25 H4
Melton Ct. SL6 25 F5
Michael Clo. SL6 24 D6
Moffey Hill. SL6 25 E1
Moneycrower Dri. SL6 25 E4
Montrose Dri. SL6 24 A5
Moor La. SL6 25 F2
Moorbridge Rd. SL6 25 G4
Moorfield Ter. SL6 25 H3
Moorlands Dri. SL6 24 A3
Moorside Clo. SL6 25 F2
Mossy Vale. SL6 25 E2
Muddy La. SL6 24 C5
Mulberry Walk. SL6 24 C3
Murrin Rd. SL6 24 C3
Napier Rd. SL6 24 B5
Newbury Dri. SL6 25 H5
Nicholsons La. SL6 25 F4
Norden Meadow. SL6 24 C6
Norden Rd. SL6 24 D6
Norfolk Park Cotts. SL6 25 F3
Norfolk Rd. SL6 25 E3
North Dean. SL6 25 F2
North Field Rd. SL6 25 F2
North Green. SL6 25 F2
North Rd. SL6 25 E4
North Star La. SL6 24 D5
North Town Clo. SL6 25 G2
North Town Mead. SL6 25 G2
North Town Moor. SL6 25 F2
North Town Rd. SL6 25 F2
Oaken Gro. SL6 24 C2
Oldacres. SL6 25 H4
Oldershaw Mews. SL6 24 C3
Oldfield Rd. SL6 25 H5
Orchard Gro. SL6 24 D4
Osney Rd. SL6 25 E1
Ostler Gate. SL6 24 C2
Park St. SL6 25 G4
Parkside. SL6 24 D2
Partridge Mead. SL6 25 F1
Pearce Clo. SL6 25 F2
Pearce Rd. SL6 25 F2
Penshurst Rd. SL6 24 D6
Penyston Rd. SL6 24 C4
Pine Clo. SL6 24 C4
Pinkneys Dri. SL6 24 A3
Pinkneys Rd. SL6 24 B2
Poplars Gro. SL6 25 H1
Portlock Rd. SL6 24 C4
Powney Rd. SL6 24 D4
Prince Andrews Clo. SL6 25 H2
Prince Andrews Rd. SL6 25 H2
Princess St. SL6 25 F5
Providence Pl. SL6 25 G4
Queen St. SL6 25 F5
Queensway. SL6 25 E2
Ray Dri. SL6 25 H4
Ray Lea Clo. SL6 25 H3
Ray Lea Rd. SL6 25 H2
Ray Meadow. SL6 25 G2
Ray Mill Rd. SL6 25 G2
Ray Mill Rd E. SL6 25 H2
Ray Mill Rd W. SL6 25 F3
Ray Park Av. SL6 25 H2
Ray Park La. SL6 25 H3
Ray Park Rd. SL6 25 H3
Ray St. SL6 25 H4
Raymond Rd. SL6 24 D4
Redriff Clo. SL6 24 D5
Reform Rd. SL6 25 H4
Reid Av. SL6 25 E6
Risborough Rd. SL6 25 F3
Riseley Rd. SL6 24 D4
Rixman Clo. SL6 24 D6
Roseleigh Clo. SL6 24 B4
Ross Rd. SL6 25 E6
Rushington Av. SL6 25 F6
Russell Ct. SL6 25 F4
Rutland Gate. SL6 24 D5
Rutland Pl. SL6 24 D5
Rutland Rd. SL6 24 D5
Sadlers Mews. SL6 25 H4
St Cloud Way. SL6 25 G4
St Ives Rd. SL6 25 G4
St Lukes Rd. SL6 25 F4
St Margarets Rd. SL6 24 B4
St Marks Cres. SL6 24 B4
St Marks Rd. SL6 24 C4
St Peters Rd. SL6 24 D1
Salters Clo. SL6 25 H4
Salters Rd. SL6 25 H4
Sandisplatt Rd. SL6 24 A5
Sandringham Rd. SL6 25 F1
Savoy Ct. SL6 25 F1
School La. SL6 25 F2
Sheephouse Rd. SL6 25 H2
Sherwood Dri. SL6 24 B5
Shifford Cres. SL6 25 E1
Shirley Rd. SL6 24 C6
Shoppenhangers Rd. SL6 25 E6
Silco Dri. SL6 25 F5
Silver Clo. SL6 24 A6
Silvertrees Dri. SL6 24 B6
Simpson Clo. SL6 25 H3
South Rd. SL6 25 F5
Spencers Clo. SL6 24 D3
Spencers Rd. SL6 24 D3
Sperling Rd. SL6 25 F2
Spring Clo. SL6 25 F1
Stafferton Way. SL6 25 G5
Stamford Rd. SL6 24 D5
Station App. SL6 25 F5
Stirling Gro. SL6 24 B3
Stonefield Park. SL6 24 D4
Summerford Ct. SL6 25 H3
Summerleaze Rd. SL6 25 G2
Sun La. SL6 25 F4
Sunderland Rd. SL6 24 B3
Sutton Clo. SL6 24 D5
Switchback Clo. SL6 24 D1
Switchback Rd Nth. SL6 25 E1
Switchback Rd Sth. SL6 24 D1
Sylvester Rd. SL6 25 E1
Tachbrook Clo. SL6 25 G3
Talbots Dri. SL6 24 B5
Tavistock Clo. SL6 24 A3
Taylors Ct. SL6 24 C3
Thames Cres. SL6 25 H1
Thatchers Dri. SL6 24 A6
The Chase. SL6 24 D1
The Crescent. SL6 25 E4
The Croft. SL6 24 D6
The Farthingales. SL6 25 H4
The Paddock. SL6 24 C1
The Pagoda. SL6 25 H2
The Ridings. SL6 24 A4
The Wicketts. SL6 24 C4
Thicket Grn. SL6 24 A4
Timbers Walk. SL6 24 B6
Tollgate. SL6 24 A5
Truro Clo. SL6 24 A4
Turpins Grn. SL6 24 B6
Twynham Rd. SL6 24 B4
Underhill Clo. SL6 25 E5
Vicarage Rd. SL6 25 F3
Victor Clo. SL6 24 C3
Waldeck Rd. SL6 25 H4
Wavell Rd. SL6 24 C5
Wayside Ms. SL6 25 F3
Webster Clo. SL6 24 B6
Webster Ct. SL6 24 D5
Welbeck Rd. SL6 24 D6
Wellhouse Rd. SL6 25 E1
Wellington Rd. SL6 24 D4
Wentworth Cres. SL6 24 C5
West Dean. SL6 25 F3
West Rd. SL6 25 E4
West St. SL6 25 F4
Westborough Rd. SL6 24 D5
Westfield Rd. SL6 24 C4
Westmead. SL6 25 F1
Westmorland Rd. SL6 24 D4
White Hart Rd. SL6 25 F4
White Rock. SL6 25 H2
Whurley Way. SL6 25 E1
Wilberforce Ms. SL6 25 F4
Winbury Ct. SL6 25 E4
Windrush Way. SL6 25 G3
Winter Hill Rd. SL6 24 A1
Woodcote. SL6 25 E5
Woodfield Dri. SL6 24 B5
Woodhurst Rd. SL6 25 H2
Woodstock Clo. SL6 25 F2
Wootton Way. SL6 24 C5
Yew Tree Clo. SL6 25 E3
York Rd. SL6 25 G5

NEWBURY

Aberbury Clo. RG14 26 C2
Abbey Clo. RG14 29 E2
Abbots Rd. RG14 29 E1
Abex Rd. RG14 27 F5
Aintree Clo. RG14 29 F2
Albert Rd. RG14 26 D4
Alder Clo. RG14 27 G4
Almond Av. RG14 26 D3
Amberley Clo. RG14 26 C4
Ampere Rd. RG14 27 E4
Andover Rd. RG14 28 B6
Angel Ct. RG14 26 D4
Apple Tree Clo. RG14 28 C3
Argyll Rd. RG14 28 D1
Arnhem Rd. RG14 27 E5
Arthur Rd. RG14 28 C1
Ascot Clo. RG14 29 F2
Ashton Rd. RG14 27 E5
Ashwood Dri. RG14 27 G4
Audley Clo. RG14 27 G3
Austen Gdns. RG14 29 F2
Avonway. RG14 27 G4
Badgers Ridge. RG20 28 A6
Bagnols Way. RG14 26 B6
Balfour Cres. RG14 28 A5
Barn Cres. RG14 28 B4
Bartholomew St. RG14 26 D6
Bartlemy Clo. RG14 28 C2
Bartlemy Rd. RG14 28 C2
Bath Rd. RG14 26 A3
Battery End. RG14 28 B4
Battle Clo. RG14 26 B3
Battle Rd. RG14 28 A4
Baysmead. RG14 28 D2
Bedford Clo. RG14 28 A5
Bell Hill. RG14 28 A6
Bell Holt. RG14 28 A5
Belvedere Dri. RG14 28 D2
Benett Clo. RG14 26 C3
Benett Gdns. RG14 26 C3
Berkeley Rd. RG14 26 C5
Birchwood Rd. RG14 27 G4
Black Bear La. RG14 26 D5
Blagden Clo. RG19 29 G3
Bledlow Clo. RG14 28 A5
Blenheim Rd. RG14 26 C5
Bodin Gdns. RG14 29 E3
Bone La. RG14 27 E5
Bonemill La. RG14 28 B1
Bostock Rd. RG14 29 E2
Boundary Rd. RG14 27 E5
Braunfels Walk. RG14 26 B6
Bridge St. RG14 26 D5
Brookway. RG14 27 H6
Bruan Rd. RG14 28 D3
Brummell Rd. RG14 26 B3
Buckingham Rd. RG14 28 C1
Bunkers Hill. RG14 28 A5
Burchell Rd. RG14 26 B3
Burys Bank Rd. RG19 29 G3
Butson Clo. RG14 26 B5
Byron Clo. RG14 28 D3
Canal Vw Rd. RG14 27 G5
Canal Walk. RG14 26 D5
Cansfield End. RG14 26 C5
Carey Clo. RG14 28 B4
Carnegie Rd. RG14 26 D6
Castle Gro. RG14 26 C3
Castle La. RG14 26 C2
Catherine Rd. RG14 29 E1
Caunter Rd. RG14 26 B3
Cavalier Clo. RG14 27 F3
Cavendish Ct. RG14 27 H3

Cedar Mt. RG14 28 D3
Chalford Rd. RG14 26 B5
Chandos Rd. RG14 28 D3
Charles St. RG14 28 B4
Charlton Pl. RG14 27 E4
Charnwood Clo. RG14 26 C3
Charter Rd. RG14 28 D3
Chaucer Cres. RG14 26 B3
Cheap St. RG14 26 D5
Cheriton Clo. RG14 29 E2
Cherry Clo. RG14 26 D3
Chester Clo. RG14 29 G2
Chesterfield Rd. RG14 28 D1
Chestnut Cres. RG14 26 D4
Cheviot Clo. RG14 28 A5
Chiltern Clo. RG14 28 A5
Christie Heights. RG14 29 E3
Christopher Ct. RG14 27 E6
Church La. RG14 26 A4
Church Rd. RG14 27 E3
Clarendon Gdns. RG14 26 D4
Clay Hill. RG14 27 G3
Cleveland Gro. RG14 26 C5
Clifton Rd. RG14 26 B6
Coachmans Clo. RG14 27 E3
Collins Clo. RG14 27 F4
Conifer Crest. RG14 28 A5
Connaught Rd. RG14 27 E5
Cope Hall La. RG14 28 A3
Coppice Clo. RG14 29 E2
Coster Clo. RG14 26 B3
Courtlands Rd. RG14 29 E2
Cowslade Rd. RG14 26 B3
Coxeter Rd. RG14 26 B3
Cranford Pl. RG14 26 C5
Craven Dene. RG14 27 F4
Craven Rd. RG14 26 B6
Crawford Pl. RG14 26 C5
Creswell Rd. RG14 27 G4
Croft La. RG14 26 C4
Croft Rd. RG14 28 D2
Cromwell Pl. RG14 26 D5
Cromwell Rd. RG14 27 F3
Cromwell Ter. RG14 26 A3
Culver Rd. RG14 28 C3
Curling Way. RG14 27 F4
Cyril Vokins Rd. RG14 27 H6
Dalby Cres. RG14 29 F2
De Montfort Rd. RG14 26 B3
Deadmans La. RG19 29 E4
Dene Way. RG14 26 D2
Denmark Rd. RG14 27 E5
Derby Rd. RG14 28 D1
Dickens Walk. RG14 29 E2
Digby Rd. RG14 26 C3
Dolman Rd. RG14 26 D3
Donnington Lodge. RG14 26 C1
Donnington Pk. RG14 26 C2
Donnington Sq. RG14 26 C3
Dormer Clo. RG14 28 B4
Doveton Way. RG14 27 E4
Dyson Clo. RG14 26 C5
Edgecombe La. RG14 27 F3
Eeklo Pl. RG14 29 E1
Elizabeth Av. RG14 28 B4
Enborne Gate. RG14 28 B1
Enborne Gro. RG14 28 C1
Enborne Pl. RG14 28 C1
Enborne Rd. RG14 28 A1
Enborne St. RG14 28 A5
Epsom Cres. RG14 29 F2
Equine Way. RG14 29 F3
Erleigh Dene. RG14 28 D2
Essex St. RG14 28 A4
Ewing Way. RG14 29 E2
Express Way. RG14 27 H6
Fairfax Pl. RG14 27 H3
Falkland Dri. RG14 28 D2
Falkland Garth. RG14 28 B4
Falkland Rd. RG14 28 B4
Faraday Rd. RG14 27 E5
Fennel Clo. RG14 27 G3
Ferrier Gro. RG14 29 E2
Fieldridge. RG14 27 F3
Fifth Rd. RG14 28 C2
Fir Tree La. RG14 27 H4
First Av. RG14 27 F4
Fleetwood Clo. RG14 27 G3
Fleming Rd. RG14 27 E4
Floreat Gdns. RG14 28 C1
Fontwell Rd. RG14 29 F1
Friars Rd. RG14 27 E3
Garden Close La. RG14 28 B5

Garford Cres. RG14 28 B3
Gaskell Ms. RG14 29 E2
Gaywood Dri. RG14 27 G4
Gilroy Clo. RG14 28 A5
Glebe Fields. RG14 27 E3
Glendale Av. RG14 28 A5
Gloucester Rd. RG14 26 B6
Goldwell Dri. RG14 26 C4
Goodwin Walk. RG14 28 A4
Goodwood Way. RG14 29 F1
Gordon Rd. RG14 27 E6
Gorselands. RG14 28 B5
Gould Clo. RG14 27 E6
Grange Ct. RG14 27 E6
Green La. RG14 26 B6
Greenham Clo. RG19 29 G3
Greenham Mill. RG14 27 E5
Greenham Rd. RG14 29 E1
Greenlands Rd. RG14 29 E2
Greyberry Copse Rd. RG19 29 G3
Groombridge Pl. RG14 26 C2
Grove Ct. RG14 29 E3
Grove Rd. RG14 26 B3
Groveland Rd. RG14 26 B3
Gwyn Clo. RG14 28 C2
Hambridge La. RG14 27 G5
Hambridge Rd. RG14 27 F6
Hamilton Ct. RG14 29 E2
Hampton Rd. RG14 28 D1
Hanover Mead. RG14 28 B4
Harrington La. RG14 27 H3
Harvest Grn. RG14 28 C1
Hawthorn Rd. RG14 26 D4
Heather Gdns. RG14 28 C3
Hector Way. RG14 27 E6
Hedgeway. RG14 27 F4
Henshaw Cres. RG14 28 B2
Herewood Clo. RG14 26 C3
*Highfield Av, Market St. RG14 26 D6
Highfield Rd. RG14 28 D2
Highwood Clo. RG14 27 F2
Hill Clo. RG14 28 B4
Hill Rd. RG14 28 B4
Holbourne Clo. RG14 28 A5
Homemead Clo. RG14 27 G4
Hopwood Clo. RG14 27 G4
Horseshoe End. RG14 29 F3
Howard Rd. RG14 29 E1
Hutton Clo. RG14 27 E4
INDUSTRIAL & RETAIL:
Castle Ind Park. RG14 27 F3
Horizon West Ind Est. RG14 27 G5
London Road Ind Est. RG14 27 E4
Newbury Business Pk. RG14 27 F4
Overbridge Ind Est. RG14 27 G5
Raceview Business Centre. RG14 27 E6
Turnpike Road Ind Est. RG14 27 G3
Jack St. RG14 26 D5
Jesmond Dene. RG14 26 C4
John Childs Clo. RG14 28 D1
Jubilee Rd. RG14 27 E6
Junction Ter. RG14 27 F5
Kelvin Rd. RG14 27 E4
Kempton Clo. RG14 29 F2
Kendrick Rd. RG14 28 B5
Kennedy Clo. RG14 28 B4
Kennet Clo. RG14 26 C5
Kennet Side. RG14 27 F5
Kersey Cres. RG14 28 B4
Kiln Rd. RG14 27 E3
Kimbers Clo. RG14 28 D5
Kimbers Dri. RG14 26 A3
Kingfisher Ct. RG14 27 G5
Kings Rd. RG14 27 E5
Kings Rd W. RG14 26 D6
Kingsbridge Rd. RG14 28 B1
Kingsland Grange. RG14 28 C3
Kingsley Clo. RG14 27 F2
Laburnham Gro. RG14 26 D4
Ladwell Clo. RG14 28 B6
Lambourn Clo. RG14 26 A2
Lamp Acres. RG14 27 F2
Larch Clo. RG14 26 B3
Laud Clo. RG14 27 G3
Leslie Southern Ct. RG14 27 E4

Lewendon Rd. RG14 26 B3
Leys Gdns. RG14 26 C4
Lime Clo. RG14 27 G4
Linden Clo. RG14 26 C4
Lingfield Rd. RG14 29 F2
Link Rd. RG14 28 D1
Lipscombe Clo. RG14 26 B5
Lisle Clo. RG14 26 D3
Livingstone Rd. RG14 27 E6
London Rd. RG14 27 E4
Long La. RG14 27 F2
Longacre. RG14 28 B2
Love La. RG14 26 C2
Lower Way. RG14 27 H4
Ludlow Clo. RG14 27 H3
Lynton Ct. RG14 26 D4
Majendie Clo. RG14 26 A3
Mallard Ct. RG14 26 C5
Malvern Ct. RG14 28 D1
Mandarin Ct. RG14 27 F6
Manor Pl. RG14 26 A3
Mansell Dri. RG14 28 A5
Mansion House St. RG14 26 D5
Maple Cres. RG14 26 D3
Marchant Clo. RG19 29 G3
Marconi Rd. RG14 27 E4
Market Pl. RG14 26 D5
Market St. RG14 26 D6
Marsh La. RG14 26 D5
Marshalls Ct. RG14 26 A3
Marston Dri. RG14 27 G3
Matchlock Mews. RG14 27 F3
Mayfair Dri. RG14 28 C1
*Mayors La, Market St. RG14 26 D6
Meadow Rd. RG14 28 D2
Meldrum Clo. RG14 28 A5
Meyrick Dri. RG14 28 A5
Middle Clo. RG14 28 B3
Middleton Ct. RG14 27 H3
Mill La. RG14 27 E5
Monks La. RG14 28 C4
Monkswood Clo. RG14 28 B3
Montague Ter. RG14 28 D2
Montgomery Rd. RG14 28 C2
Monument Clo. RG14 28 B4
Moor La. RG14 26 B4
Mount Clo. RG14 29 E2
Mountbatten Clo. RG14 27 H4
Naseby Rise. RG14 27 G3
New Rd, Greenham. RG19 29 G3
New R, Newbury. RG14 29 F1
Newbold Rd. RG14 26 B3
Newbury By-Pass. RG14 26 A2
Newport Clo. RG14 29 F2
Newport Rd. RG14 27 E4
Newtown Rd. RG14 28 D1
Normay Rise. RG14 28 A5
Northbrook St. RG14 26 D5
Northcroft La. RG14 26 D5
Northern Av. RG14 26 D2
Northway. RG14 27 E6
Northwood Dri. RG14 27 F3
Norton Clo. RG14 28 A5
Oak Dri. RG14 28 C1
Oaken Gro. RG14 28 B2
Oakley Rd. RG14 27 G4
Oakridge Clo. RG14 26 B4
Oddfellows Rd. RG14 26 D5
Old Newtown Rd. RG14 28 D1
Orchard Clo. RG14 27 F3
Orchardene. RG14 27 E4
Orts Rd. RG14 27 E5
Owen Rd. RG14 27 E2
Oxford Rd. RG14 26 D3
Oxford St. RG14 26 D4
Paddock Rd. RG14 26 D4
Park End. RG14 26 D4
Park La. RG14 26 D4
Park St. RG14 26 D4
Park Way. RG14 26 D4
Parsons Clo. RG14 26 B6
Pear Tree La. RG14 27 F2
Peckmoor Dri. RG19 29 G3
Pelican La. RG14 26 D4
Pembroke Rd. RG14 26 D3
Penn Rd. RG14 26 B3
Penrose Clo. RG14 28 A4
Pigeon Farm Rd. RG19 29 G3
Pike St. RG14 27 F4

Pinchington La. RG14 29 E3
Pindar Pl. RG14 27 H3
Pine Ridge. RG14 27 G3
Plumpton Rd. RG14 29 F2
Pond Clo. RG14 28 B3
Poplar Pl. RG14 26 D3
Porchester Rd. RG14 28 D1
Porter End. RG14 29 F2
Posting House Ms. RG14 26 C4
Pound La. RG14 26 A3
Pound St. RG14 26 C6
Preston Pl. RG14 27 G3
Priory Pl. RG14 29 E4
Priory Rd. RG14 28 D2
Pritchard Clo. RG19 29 G3
Prospect Pl. RG14 28 D1
Puffers Way. RG14 26 B6
Queens Rd. RG14 27 E6
Racecourse Rd. RG14 29 E1
Railway Rd. RG14 27 E6
Rectory Clo. RG14 28 D1
Redfield Clo. RG14 27 G4
Regnum Dri. RG14 27 E3
Remembrance Rd. RG14 28 C1
Ring Rd. RG14 27 E5
Robertson Clo. RG14 29 E3
Robins Clo. RG14 28 D3
Rockingham Rd. RG14 26 C6
Roebuts Clo. RG14 28 D2
Rokeby Clo. RG14 29 E3
Round End. RG14 28 B5
Rowan Dri. RG14 26 D3
Rupert Rd. RG14 28 D3
Russell Rd. RG14 26 B5
Saffron Clo. RG14 26 C5
St Davids Rd. RG14 26 C6
St Donats Pl. RG14 29 E1
St Georges Av. RG14 26 C6
St Johns Rd. RG14 27 E4
St Marys Rd. RG14 27 E4
St Michaels Rd. RG14 26 C6
St Nicholas Rd. RG14 26 C6
St Richards Rd. RG14 27 G4
Salcombe Rd. RG14 28 C1
Sandleford Link. RG14 29 E1
Sandleford Rise. RG14 28 D3
Sandown Way. RG14 29 F3
Sayers Clo. RG14 29 F2
Sedgefield Rd. RG14 29 F2
Shaw Farm Rd. RG14 27 E2
Shaw Hill. RG14 27 E3
Shaw Rd. RG14 27 E4
Sherrardmead. RG14 27 E3
Shop La. RG14 26 C2
Sidestrand Rd. RG14 28 C3
Skipings Clo. RG14 28 A4
Skyllings. RG14 28 A4
Smallridge. RG20 28 A6
Sorrel Clo. RG14 26 B4
Spa Meadow Clo. RG19 29 G3
Speen Hill Clo. RG14 26 B4
Speen La. RG14 26 A3
Speen Lodge Ct. RG14 26 B4
Speen Pl. RG14 26 B4
Spencer Rd. RG14 28 B5
Springfield La. RG14 29 E3
Stable Ct. RG14 27 E2
Stanley Rd. RG14 27 E6
Stapleton Clo. RG14 28 A4
Starting Gate. RG14 29 E2
Station Rd, Newbury. RG14 26 D6
Station Rd, Speen. RG14 26 A3
Stirrup Clo. RG14 29 E3
Stoney La. RG14 27 G3
Strawberry Hill. RG14 26 C4
Stuart Rd. RG14 28 A4
Sunley Clo. RG14 28 C5
Sunnyside. RG14 26 C2
Sutherlands. RG14 28 C4
Sutton Rd. RG14 26 B3
Swan Ct. RG14 26 D5
Sycamore Rise. RG14 26 B3
Sylvester Clo. RG14 26 B3
Talbot Clo. RG14 26 D4
Tarn La. RG14 28 C2
The Baxendales. RG14 29 F1
The Brambles. RG14 26 D4
The Broadway. RG14 26 D4
The Chase. RG14 26 C1
The Drive. RG14 28 C2

The Folly. RG14 29 E1
The Gabriels. RG14 28 B5
The Glade. RG14 28 C3
The Grange. RG14 28 A6
The Halters. RG14 29 F3
The Hampdens. RG14 28 A4
The Hollies. RG14 28 B5
The Laurels. RG14 28 D3
The Marlows. RG14 28 D3
The Mews. RG14 26 B5
The Nightingales. RG14 29 E2
The Paddock. RG14 27 F6
The Sydings. RG14 26 A3
The Triangle. RG19 29 E4
The Water Meadows. RG19 27 E3
Three Acre Rd. RG14 28 C3
Trout Walk. RG14 27 F3
Tudor Rd. RG14 29 E1
Turnpike Rd. RG14 27 G3
Two Rivers Way. RG14 27 G5
Tydehams. RG14 28 C3
Valley Rd. RG14 28 B3
*Victoria Gdns, St Marys Rd. RG14 27 E4
Villiers Way. RG14 28 A4
Vine Ct. RG14 29 E1
Waldergrave Pl. RG14 26 D5
Waller Dri. RG14 27 H3
Walton Way. RG14 27 F3
Wansey Gdns. RG14 27 G3
Warren Rd. RG14 28 B5
Warwick Dri. RG14 29 F1
Water La. RG19 29 G3
Waterside Ct. RG14 27 F5
Well Meadow. RG14 27 E3
Wellington Clo. RG14 27 F3
Wendan Rd. RG14 28 D2
Wentworth Ct. RG14 28 C3
West Mills. RG14 26 D5
West Mills Yd. RG14 26 D5
West St. RG14 26 D5
Westbourne Ter. RG14 26 D4
Western Av. RG14 26 C4
Western End. RG14 26 B6
Westfield Way. RG14 28 C1
Westgate Ct. RG14 28 C1
Westgate Rd. RG14 28 C1
Westlands Rd. RG14 29 E2
Westmead Dri. RG14 28 D2
Westwood Rd. RG14 29 F2
Wharf Rd. RG14 26 D5
Wharf St. RG14 26 D5
Wheatlands La. RG14 28 A4
Wheatsheaf La. RG14 27 E3
Willow Clo. RG14 28 D1
Willowmead Clo. RG14 28 A6
Wilmot Walk. RG14 28 A4
Winchcombe Rd. RG14 26 D5
Windsor Rd. RG14 29 F2
Winterton Dri. RG14 26 A3
Wood Ridge. RG14 28 C3
Woodside. RG14 28 B3
Wormersley Rd. RG19 29 G3
Wyndham Rd. RG14 27 G3
Yates Copse. RG14 27 H3
Yew Gate. RG14 26 D2
York Clo. RG14 29 E1
York Rd. RG14 29 E1
Young Cres. RG19 29 H2

OLD WINDSOR

Albany Rd. SL4 45 A3
Albert Rd. SL4 45 A2
Ashbrook Rd. SL4 45 B5
Aylesworth Spur. SL4 45 B5
Burfield Rd. SL4 45 A4
Cell Farm Av. SL4 45 B3
Church Rd. SL4 45 B3
Clayhall La. SL4 45 A3
Coppice Dri. TW19 45 D5
Cornwall Rd. SL4 45 A4
Crimp Hill. SL4 45 A4
Crimp Hill Rd. SL4 45 A5
Datchet Rd. SL4 45 A2
Fairfield App. TW19 45 D4
Fairfield Rd. TW19 45 D4
Farm Dri. SL4 45 C4
Follet Clo. SL4 45 B4
Friary Rd. TW19 45 C5
Garson La. TW19 45 D5

Glebe Rd. SL4 45 B3
Gregory Dri. SL4 45 B4
Grove Clo. SL4 45 C5
Hartley Copse. SL4 45 A4
Harwood Gdns. SL4 45 B5
Keppel Spur. SL4 45 B5
King Johns Clo. TW19 45 C4
Kingsbury Dri. SL4 45 B4
Kingswood Creek.
   TW19 45 D3
Lyndwood Dri. SL4 45 A4
Magna Carta La. TW19 45 B4
Malt House Clo. SL4 45 C5
Manor Farm Cotts. SL4 45 B3
Meadow Clo. SL4 45 B4
Meadow Way. SL4 45 B4
Millers La. SL4 45 A4
Mills Spur. SL4 45 B5
Newton Ct. SL4 45 B4
Newton La. SL4 45 B4
Nursery Way. TW19 45 C4
Old Ferry Dri. TW19 45 C4
Orchard Rd. SL4 45 B4
Ouseley Rd. SL4 45 C5
Park Av. TW19 45 D3
Pelling Hill. SL4 45 B5
Pollards Clo. SL4 45 B3
Priest Hill. SL4 45 C6
Queens Clo. SL4 45 B3
Ricardo Rd. SL4 45 B4
Riverside. TW19 45 C5
Robin Willis Way. SL4 45 A4
St Andrews Clo. SL4 45 A4
St Lukes Rd. SL4 45 A4
St Peters Clo. SL4 45 B3
Saxon Way. SL4 45 B4
Southlea Rd. SL4 45 A2
Straight Rd. SL4 45 A3
The Avenue. SL4 45 B3
The Crofters. SL4 45 A4
The Drive. TW19 45 D3
The Embankment.
   TW19 45 C5
The Friary. SL4 45 C4
The Grange. SL4 45 B3
Tudor La. SL4 45 C5
Tyle Pl. SL4 45 A3
Walpole Rd. SL4 45 B5
Warrington Spur. SL4 45 B5
Wharf Rd. TW19 45 C5
William Ellis Clo. SL4 45 A4
Windsor Rd. SL4 45 C6

PANGBOURNE

Aston Clo. RG8 30 C4
Bere Court Rd. RG8 30 A5
Bourne Rd. RG8 30 C3
Breedons Hill. RG8 30 B3
Briars Clo. RG8 30 D3
Bucknell Av. RG8 30 C3
Cedar Dri. RG8 30 B4
Chiltern Walk. RG8 30 C3
Church Rd. RG8 30 B3
Coach House Ct. RG8 30 C3
Courtlands Hill. RG8 30 B4
Duchess Clo. RG8 30 B1
Dunluce Gdns. RG8 30 C2
Eastfield Rd. RG8 30 B2
Flowers Hill. RG8 30 B4
Grahame Av. RG8 30 C4
Green La. RG8 30 A4
Hardwick Rd. RG8 30 B1
Hartslock Ct. RG8 30 A2
High St,
   Pangbourne. RG8 30 B3
High St,
   Whitchurch. RG8 30 B1
Hillside. RG8 30 C1
Horseshoe Pk. RG8 30 C3
Horseshoe Rd. RG8 30 C3
INDUSTRIAL & RETAIL:
   Horseshoe Park Ind Est.
   RG8 30 C4
Kennedy Dri. RG8 30 C4
Manor Rd. RG8 30 B1
Meadow La. RG8 30 C3
Meadowside Rd. RG8 30 B3
Orchard Pl. RG8 30 C3
Pages Gdns. RG8 30 C3
Pangbourne Hill. RG8 30 A4
Pangbourne Mws. RG8 30 C3
Purley Rise. RG8 30 D3
Purley Way. RG8 30 C3
Reading Rd. RG8 30 B3
Riverview Rd. RG8 30 B3
St James Clo. RG8 30 B3
Shooters Hill. RG8 30 A2
Short St. RG8 30 C3
Station Rd. RG8 30 B3
Stokes Vw. RG8 30 B3
Strachay Clo. RG8 30 B6
Sulham La. RG8 30 D4
Swanston Field. RG8 30 C1
Sycamore Ct. RG8 30 B3
Thames Av. RG8 30 B2
The Laurels. RG8 30 C3
The Moors. RG8 30 B3
The Square. RG8 30 B3
The Street. RG8 30 B5
The Wharf. RG8 30 B2
Tidmarsh Rd. RG8 30 A4
Whitchurch Bri. RG8 30 C2
Whitchurch Rd. RG8 30 B2
Wilder Av. RG8 30 D3
Willow Ct. RG8 30 B3
Woodview Rd. RG8 30 C3

PURLEY

Addiscombe Chase.
   RG31 31 A3
Albert Illsley Clo. RG31 31 B6
Alford Clo. RG30 31 C6
Allison Gdns. RG8 31 A1
Andover Clo. RG31 31 C5
Apple Clo. RG31 31 A3
Armour Hill. RG31 31 B5
Armour Rd. RG31 31 B5
Armour Wk. RG31 31 B5
Ashton Clo. RG31 31 B6
Avington Clo. RG31 31 A6
Aylsham Clo. RG30 6 D6
Back La. RG7 31 A5
Barbrook Clo. RG31 31 C3
Barefoot Clo. RG31 31 A5
Beatty Dri. RG30 31 C6
Belleisle. RG8 31 A2
Beverley Rd. RG31 31 B6
Blundells Rd. RG30 31 C6
Bowfell Clo. RG31 31 A4
Bowling Green La. RG8 31 A2
Bracken Clo. RG31 31 A5
Brading Way. RG8 31 B1
Bradwell Rd. RG31 31 B3
Brendon Clo. RG30 31 D5
Brierley Pl. RG31 31 A3
Brooksby Rd. RG31 31 B4
Bryant Pl. RG8 31 A2
Bungalow Dri. RG31 31 C6
Calder Clo. RG30 31 D6
Carew Clo. RG31 31 A3
Carlisle Rd. RG31 31 C4
Causmans Way. RG31 31 B5
Cecil Aldin Dri. RG31 31 A2
Chapel Hill. RG31 31 A6
Chelsea Clo. RG30 31 D6
Chepstow Rd. RG31 31 B6
Chestnut Gro. RG8 31 C1
Chichester Rd. RG30 31 D6
Childrey Way. RG31 31 A6
Chiltern Vw. RG8 31 B2
Church End La. RG30 31 D6
Church Mews. RG8 31 B1
Clanfield Cres. RG31 31 B4
Clay Clo. RG31 31 A5
Clements Mead. RG31 31 A6
Clevedon Rd. RG31 31 C3
Coalport Way. RG30 31 D6
Colyton Way. RG8 31 B1
Condor Clo. RG31 31 A3
Coniston Dri. RG30 31 D4
Copse Clo. RG31 31 B3
Cornwall Clo. RG31 31 A3
*Cornwall Coppice,
   Meadowside. RG31 31 A5
Corwen Rd. RG30 6 C6
Cotswold Way. RG31 31 A4
Cranmer Clo. RG31 31 A3
Crescent Rd. RG31 31 B5
Cromer Clo. RG31 31 A6
Dark La. RG31 31 A4
Dartington Clo. RG30 31 D6
Delaney Clo. RG30 31 D6
Delft Clo. RG30 31 D6
Dell Rd. RG31 31 B5
Denby Way. RG30 31 D5
Derwent Av. RG30 31 D4
Devonshire Gdns.
   RG31 31 A3
Downing Rd. RG31 31 B6
Downs Way. RG31 31 A4
Dresden Way. RG31 31 D5
Dudley Clo. RG31 31 C5
Dudley Mews. RG31 31 C5
Duncan Gdns. RG8 31 B2
Dunstall Clo. RG31 31 C6
Durrant Way. RG31 31 C3
Edenhall Clo. RG31 31 C3
Elder Clo. RG31 31 A6
Elizabeth Ct. RG30 31 C6
Elmstone Dri. RG31 31 B5
Elsley Rd. RG31 31 C4
Elstree Clo. RG31 31 C4
Elyham. RG8 31 A2
Fairford Rd. RG31 31 A5
Farm Clo. RG8 31 B1
Farmiloe Clo. RG8 31 B2
Felton Way. RG31 31 B6
Fern Glen. RG31 31 B5
Ferndale Clo. RG31 31 C3
Filbert Dri. RG31 31 A6
Fircroft Clo. RG31 31 B5
Five Acre. RG31 31 A5
Forest Hill. RG30 31 D4
Fulbrook Cres. RG30 31 B3
Gipsy La. RG30 31 D5
Glebe Rd. RG8 31 A1
Goodliffe Gdns. RG31 31 B3
Grasmere Av. RG30 31 D4
Gratwicke Rd. RG31 31 C6
Greenacre Mt. RG30 31 C6
Gwynne Clo. RG31 31 B3
Halcyon Ter. RG31 31 D6
Hambleberry Ct. RG31 31 B6
Hartslock Way. RG31 31 B5
Hawthornes. RG31 31 A4
Hayfield Clo. RG31 31 A6
Hazel Rd. RG8 31 B2
Hazelwood Clo. RG31 31 B6
Heathway. RG31 31 B6
Highfield Rd. RG31 31 A2
Highworth Way. RG31 31 A5
Hillview Clo. RG31 31 A4
Hirstwood. RG30 31 C5
Holford Clo. RG31 31 B6
Holkham Clo. RG30 31 D6
Home Croft. RG31 31 A5
Hornbeam Clo. RG30 31 B2
Hornsea Clo. RG30 31 C6
Huckleberry Clo. RG8 31 B2
Huscarle Way. RG31 31 A3
Ivy Bank. RG31 31 A5
Juniper Way. RG31 31 B4
Kentwood Clo. RG30 31 C6
Kentwood Hill. RG31 31 C6
Kernham Dri. RG31 31 A3
Kirkfell Clo. RG31 31 A4
Knowsley Rd. RG31 31 A3
Lambourn Clo. RG31 31 B6
Lamorna Cres. RG31 31 A5
Larissa Clo. RG31 31 C5
Larkswood Clo. RG31 31 C4
Laurel Rd. RG31 31 A6
Laytom Rise. RG31 31 A3
Lemart Clo. RG30 31 C6
Lilac Clo. RG8 31 B2
Lister Clo. RG8 31 A1
Little Heath Rd. RG31 31 A6
Little Oaks Dri. RG31 31 B6
Long La. RG31 31 A3
Longleat Dri. RG31 31 A4
Lower Armour Rd.
   RG31 31 C5
Lower Elmstone Dri.
   RG31 31 B5
Lucey Clo. RG31 31 A4
Lyme Gro. RG31 31 B6
Lytham End. RG31 31 A3
Mapledurham Dri. RG8 31 B1
Mapledurham Vw.
   RG31 31 C4
Marling Clo. RG31 31 B4
Marshall Clo. RG31 31 B2
Marten Pl. RG31 31 A3
Meadowside. RG31 31 A5
Menpes Rd. RG31 31 B3
Midwinter Clo. RG30 31 D6
Minton Clo. RG30 31 D6
Myrtle Clo. RG31 31 B3
Nevis Rd. RG31 31 B3
New Hill. RG8 31 B2
Newbery Clo. RG31 31 C5
Norcot Rd. RG30 31 C6
Normanstead Rd. RG31 31 A6
Nursery Gdns. RG8 31 A1
Oak Tree Copse. RG31 31 C4
Oak Tree Rd. RG31 31 B4
Oak Tree Walk. RG8 31 B1
Oak View. RG31 31 B6
Oakdale Clo. RG31 31 A6
Oakham Clo. RG31 31 C4
Old Farm Cres. RG31 31 A4
Oldean Clo. RG31 31 B5
Orchard Clo. RG31 31 A2
Oregon Av. RG31 31 B3
Overdown Rd. RG31 31 A5
Oxford Rd. RG30 31 A1
Park Walk. RG30 31 B1
Parkhill Dri. RG31 31 C4
Pierces Hill. RG31 31 B5
Pikeshaw Way. RG31 31 B5
Polsted Rd. RG31 31 C5
Portmeirion Gdns.
   RG30 31 D5
Pottery Rd. RG30 31 D5
Primrose Clo. RG8 31 B1
Prince William Dri.
   RG31 31 A5
Purley La. RG8 31 A1
Purley Rise. RG8 31 A1
Purley Village St. RG8 30 A1
Recreation Rd. RG30 31 C6
Redwood Way. RG31 31 A4
Ridgemount Clo. RG31 31 A4
Riley Rd. RG31 31 D6
Rissington Clo. RG31 31 C4
River Gdns. RG8 31 C2
Rodway Rd. RG30 31 D5
Roebuck Rise. RG31 31 A3
Rosemead Av. RG31 31 A3
Rydal Av. RG30 31 D4
Sage Rd. RG31 31 B3
St Marys Av. RG8 31 B1
Sanctuary Clo. RG30 31 D6
Saunders Ct. RG8 31 A2
Scafell Clo. RG31 31 A4
School Rd. RG31 31 C6
Sheraton Dri. RG31 31 A6
Sherwood Pl. RG8 31 A2
Sherwood Rise. RG8 31 A2
Shipton Clo. RG31 31 B4
Simons Clo. RG31 31 B2
Skerritt Way. RG8 31 B2
Skilton Rd. RG31 31 B4
Southerndene Clo.
   RG31 31 B4
Spode Clo. RG30 31 D6
Staddlestone Clo. RG31 31 A4
Staffordshire Clo. RG30 31 D6
Swansea Ter. RG31 31 C5
Swinbrook Clo. RG31 31 B3
Swiss Cottage Clo.
   RG31 31 A6
Talbot Way. RG31 31 A3
Taynton Wk. RG1 33 E5
Thames Reach. RG8 31 B2
The Beeches. RG31 31 C3
The Cedars. RG31 31 B5
The Glade. RG8 31 B2
The Holt. RG8 31 B2
The Hydes. RG31 31 A3
The Knoll. RG31 31 A5
The Sadlers. RG31 31 A5
The Short. RG31 31 B1
Theobald Grn. RG31 31 B6
Thirlmere Av. RG31 31 D4
Thistledown. RG31 31 A5
Tilling Clo. RG31 31 A4
Trelawney Dri. RG31 31 A5
Trenthams Clo. RG31 31 A2
Tring Rd. RG31 31 B4
Tuscan Clo. RG30 31 D6
Tylers Pl. RG30 31 D6
Ullswater Dri. RG31 31 C3
Vale Cres. RG30 31 D5
Ventnor Rd. RG31 31 B6
Victoria Rd. RG31 31 B6
Walnut Way. RG31 31 A4
Wandhope Way. RG31 31 A4
Warborough Av. RG31 31 A6
Warbreck Dri. RG31 31 A3
Wardle Av. RG31 31 B5
Warley Rise. RG31 31 A3
Waterside Dri. RG8 31 B2
Weald Rise. RG30 31 D5
Wealden Way. RG30 31 D6
Wedgwood Way. RG30 31 D6
Welland Clo. RG31 31 A5
Western Oaks. RG31 31 D4
Westridge Av. RG8 31 A1
Westwood Glen. RG31 31 A6
Westwood Rd. RG31 31 B5
Westwood Row. RG31 31 B4
Wheeler Ct. RG31 31 C5
White Lodge Clo. RG31 31 A3
Winston Way. RG7 31 A1
Wintringham Way. RG8 31 B1
Wyre Ct. RG31 31 A3

READING

Abattoirs Rd. RG1 32 C2
Abbey Sq. RG1 33 E3
Abbey St. RG1 33 E3
Abbots Walk. RG1 33 E3
Acacia Rd. RG1 33 F4
Addington Rd. RG1 33 F5
Addison Rd. RG1 32 C1
Admirals Ct. RG2 32 D5
Albany Rd. RG30 32 A3
Albion Ter. RG1 33 E4
Alexandra Rd. RG1 33 G5
Alfred St. RG1 32 C3
Allcroft Rd. RG1 33 E5
Alpine St. RG1 32 D5
Ambrose Pl. RG1 32 C3
Amersham Rd. RG4 33 F1
Amity Rd. RG1 33 G3
Amity St. RG1 33 G3
Anglers Way. RG1 33 F3
Anstey Rd. RG1 32 C4
Arbour Clo.RG1 32 C6
Ardler Rd. RG4 33 E1
Argyle Rd. RG1 32 B3
Argyle St. RG1 32 B3
Armadale Ct. RG30 32 A3
*Arthur Pl,
   Orts Rd. RG1 33 F3
Artillery Mews. RG30 32 A4
Ashley Rd. RG1 32 B5
Ashmere Ter. RG30 32 A2
Audley St. RG30 32 A2
Avebury Sq. RG1 33 G5
Aveley Walk. RG2 33 E5
Avon Pl. RG1 33 G3
Baker St. RG1 32 C4
Barn Clo. RG30 32 A6
Barnstaple Rd. RG1 32 D4
Barnwood Clo. RG30 32 A2
Barnwood Rd. RG30 32 B2
Baron Ct. RG30 32 A4
Barrington Way. RG1 32 B5
Barry Pl. RG1 32 C2
Basingstoke Rd. RG2 33 E6
Bath Rd. RG30 32 A5
Battle St. RG1 32 B3
Baydon Dri. RG1 32 B5
Beck Ct. RG1 33 F5
Bedford Rd. RG1 32 C3
Belle Vue Rd. RG1 32 C4
Belle Vue Ter. RG1 32 B4
Belmont Rd. RG30 32 A4
*Bembridge Pl,
   Kings Rd. RG1 33 E3
Benyon Ct. RG1 32 B4
Benyon Ct Mews. RG1 32 B5
Beresford Rd. RG30 32 B3
Berkeley Av. RG1 32 B5
Berkeley Ct. RG1 32 C4
Betam Rd. RG1 33 F3
Bexley Ct. RG30 32 A4
Biko Ct. RG1 33 F3
Blagrave St. RG1 32 D2
Blakes Cotts. RG1 33 E3
Blenheim Gdns. RG1 33 G5
Blenheim Rd. RG1 33 G4
Blyth Walk. RG2 33 E5
Body Rd. RG1 32 C4
Boston Av. RG1 32 C5
Boult St. RG1 33 E4
Boults Walk. RG2 33 E6
Bourne Av. RG2 33 E6

*Bourne-Stevens Clo,
  East St. RG1 33 E4,
Brackstone Clo. RG4 33 E1
Briants Av. RG4 33 F1
Bridge St,
  Caversham. RG4 32 C1
Bridge St,
  Reading. RG1 32 D3
Brigham Rd. RG1 32 D1
Britten Rd. RG1 32 D6
Broad St. RG1 32 D3
Brocksett Clo. RG30 32 D3
Brook Lea. RG4 33 F1
Brook St West. RG1 32 D4
Brownlow Rd. RG1 32 B4
Brunswick Hill. RG1 32 B4
Brunswick St. RG1 32 B4
Bulmershe Rd. RG1 33 H4
Burford Ct. RG1 32 C3
Butter Market. RG1 32 D3
Cambridge St. RG1 32 B3
Canal Way. RG1 33 F3
Cannon St. RG1 32 B3
Cardiff Rd. RG1 32 B2
Cardigan Gdns. RG1 33 G5
Cardigan Rd. RG1 33 G4
Cardinal Clo. RG4 32 D1
Carey St. RG1 32 D3
Carnarvon Rd. RG1 33 G4
Caroline Ct. RG1 32 B4
Caroline St. RG1 32 C3
Carsdale Clo. RG1 32 B5
Castle Cres. RG1 32 C4
Castle Hill. RG1 32 C4
Castle St. RG1 32 C4
Catherine St. RG30 32 A3
Caversham Rd. RG1 32 C1
Champion Rd. RG4 33 E1
Chain St. RG1 32 D3
Chancery Mews. RG1 32 C1
Charles St. RG1 32 C1
Charndon Clo. RG1 33 E5
Chatham St. RG1 32 C3
Cheapside. RG1 32 D3
Chester St. RG30 32 A2
Chesterman St. RG1 33 E5
Cholmeley Pl. RG1 33 G3
Cholmeley Rd. RG1 33 G3
Cholmeley Ter. RG1 33 G3
Christchurch Ct. RG2 33 E6
Christchurch Gdns. RG2 33 E6
Christchurch Rd. RG2 33 E6
Church St. RG1 32 D4
Cintra Av. RG2 33 F6
Cintra Clo. RG2 33 F6
Claydon Ct. RG4 32 D1
Clent Rd. RG2 33 E6
Clifton St. RG1 32 C3
Coldicut St. RG4 33 E1
Coley Av. RG1 32 B5
Coley Hill. RG1 32 C4
Coley Park Rd. RG1 32 C4
Coley Pl. RG1 32 C4
College Rd. RG6 33 H4
Collis St. RG2 32 D5
Connaught Clo. RG30 32 A4
Connaught Rd. RG30 32 A4
Coventry Rd. RG1 33 G3
Cow La. RG1 32 B2
Cowper Way. RG30 32 A6
Cranbury Rd. RG30 32 A4
Craven Rd. RG1 33 F4
Cremyll Rd. RG1 32 C1
Crendon Ct. RG4 32 D1
Crescent Rd. RG1 33 H5
Cross St. RG1 32 D3
Crossland Rd. RG1 33 E4
Crown Pl. RG1 33 E4
Crown St. RG1 33 E4
Culver Rd. RG6 33 H4
Cumberland Rd. RG1 33 G3
Curzon St. RG30 32 A3
Dale Rd. RG2 32 D5
De Beauvoir Rd. RG1 33 G4
De Bohun Rd. RG1 33 E2
De Montfort Rd. RG1 33 G4
Deans Farm. RG4 33 F1
Deansgate Rd. RG1 32 D4
Deepdene Clo. RG1 32 B4
Denbigh Pl. RG1 32 C1
Denmark Rd. RG1 33 F4
Derby St. RG1 32 C3
Dickens Clo. RG4 33 F1
Donnington Gdns. RG1 33 G4

Donnington Rd. RG1 33 G4
Dorothy St. RG1 32 D4
Dover St. RG1 32 C4
Downshire Sq. RG1 32 B4
Duke St. RG1 33 E3
*Dusseldorf Way,
  Broad St Mall. RG1 32 D3
Earley Pl. RG1 32 D3
East St. RG1 33 E4
Eastern Av. RG1 33 G4
Eaton Pl. RG1 32 C3
Edenham Cres. RG1 32 A5
Edgehill St. RG1 33 E5
Edinburgh Rd. RG30 32 A3
Eldon Pl. RG1 33 F4
Eldon Rd. RG1 33 F3
Eldon Sq. RG1 33 F4
Eldon Ter. RG1 33 F4
Elgar Rd. RG2 32 D5
Elgar Rd Sth. RG2 32 D6
Elizabeth Walk. RG2 33 E5
Elliots Way. RG4 32 D1
Elm Lodge Av. RG30 32 A3
Elm Park Ct. RG30 32 A4
Elm Park Rd. RG30 32 A4
Elmhurst Rd. RG1 33 F6
Epping Clo. RG1 32 C4
Epsom Ct. RG1 32 B5
Erleigh Rd. RG1 33 F4
Essex St. RG2 33 E5
Farringdon Ct. RG1 33 G4
Fatherson Rd. RG1 33 F4
Field Rd. RG1 32 C4
Filey Rd. RG1 33 G3
Firs La. RG30 32 A6
Florence Ct. RG30 32 A5
Florence Walk. RG1 33 F3
Florida Ct. RG1 32 B4
Fobney St. RG1 32 D4
Forbury Rd. RG1 33 E3
Forge Clo. RG4 33 F1
*Foundry P,
  Katesgrove La. RG1 32 D4
*Foxglove Gdns,
  Cannon St. RG1 32 B3
Foxhill Rd. RG1 33 G5
Francis St. RG1 32 C3
Franklin St. RG1 32 C3
Fraser Clo. RG1 32 C1
Freshwater Rd. RG1 33 F2
Friar St. RG1 32 D3
Froxfield Av. RG1 32 B5
Fulham Rd. RG2 32 D4
Garnet Hill. RG1 32 C4
Garnet St. RG1 32 C4
Garrard St. RG1 32 D3
Gas Works Rd. RG1 33 F3
George St,
  Lwr Caversham. RG4 33 E2
George St,
  Reading. RG1 32 B3
Glebe Rd. RG1 33 E6
Glenbeigh Ter. RG1 32 B4
Gloucester Ct. RG30 32 A4
Gloucester Rd. RG30 32 A4
Goldsmid Rd. RG1 32 B3
Gosbrook Rd. RG4 33 E1
Gower St. RG1 32 C4
Granby Ct. RG1 33 G4
Granby Gdns. RG1 33 G4
Great Knollys St. RG1 32 B3
Greenlea Clo. RG1 32 A5
Greyfriars Rd. RG1 32 D3
Greys Ct. RG1 32 D3
Gun St. RG1 32 D3
Hagley Rd. RG2 33 E6
Hamilton Rd. RG1 33 G4
Harley Rd. RG4 32 D1
Harrow Ct. RG1 32 B4
Harry Tee Ct. RG1 33 F3
Hart St. RG1 32 B3
Hatherley Rd. RG1 33 G4
Haven Ct. RG1 32 B4
Hay Rd. RG1 32 C6
Haywood Ct. RG1 33 G4
Henry St. RG1 32 D4
Heron Island. RG4 33 E1
Heron Way. RG1 32 B6
High St. RG1 32 D3
Highgrove St. RG1 33 F5
Highgrove Ter. RG1 33 E5
Hilcot Rd. RG30 32 A3
Hill Rd. RG1 32 D5

Hodsoll Rd. RG1 32 C2
Holybrook Rd. RG1 32 C5
*Hosier St,
  St Marys Butts. RG1 32 D3
Howard St. RG1 32 C3
Hungerford Dri. RG1 32 B5
Huntley Ct. RG1 33 G4
INDUSTRIAL & RETAIL:
Broad St Mall. RG1 32 C3
Cardiff Rd Ind Est.
  RG1 32 B2
Forbury Park Ind Est
  RG4 33 F3
Paddock Rd Ind Est.
  RG4 33 F1
Kidbys Ind Est. RG1 32 C5
Reading Link
  Business Pk. RG2 32 C6
Suttons Business Park.
  RG6 33 H2
The Oracle Shopping
  Centre. RG1 32 D3
James St. RG1 32 B3
Janson Ct. RG1 32 C4
Jesse Ter. RG1 32 C4
Johannes Ct. RG30 32 A4
Josephine Ct. RG30 32 A4
Jubilee Sq. RG1 33 E4
Junction Rd. RG1 33 G4
Katesgrove La. RG1 32 D4
Kenavon Dri. RG1 33 E3
Kendrick Rd. RG1 33 E4
Kenilworth Av. RG30 32 A6
Kennet Side. RG1 33 F3
Kennet St. RG1 33 E3
Kensington Rd. RG1 32 A4
Kent Rd. RG30 32 A4
Kimberley Clo. RG1 32 A5
King St. RG1 32 D3
Kingfisher Pl. RG1 33 E2
Kings Meadow Rd. RG1 33 E2
Kings Rd,
  Lwr Caversham. RG4 33 E1
Kings Rd,
  Reading. RG1 33 E3
*Kings Walk,
  King St. RG1 32 D3
Kings Wood Rd. RG30 32 A4
*Kingsgate Pl,
  Kingsgate St. RG1 33 G3
Kingsgate St. RG1 33 G3
Kinver Walk. RG1 33 E5
Lancaster Clo. RG1 33 F5
Lancing Clo. RG1 32 A4
Laud Clo. RG1 32 D5
Leopold Walk. RG1 33 F3
Lesford Rd. RG1 32 B6
Lesley Ct. RG30 32 A4
Letcombe St. RG1 32 D4
Lima Ct. RG1 32 B4
Little St. RG1 32 B3
Littlecote Dri. RG1 32 B5
Liverpool Rd. RG1 33 G3
Livery Clo. RG1 33 E4
Lock Pl. RG1 33 F3
London Rd. RG1 33 E4
London St. RG1 32 D4
Lorne Pl. RG1 32 B3
Lorne St. RG1 32 B3
Loverock Rd. RG30 32 A2
Lower Brook St. RG1 32 D4
Lower Field Rd. RG1 32 C4
Lower Mount. RG1 33 F5
Lydford Rd. RG1 33 G5
Lynden Mews RG2 32 D5
Lynmouth Rd. RG1 32 D2
Maitland Rd. RG1 32 B4
Maldon Clo. RG30 32 A4
Mallard Row. RG1 32 D4
Malthouse La. RG1 32 C3
Maltings Pl. RG1 33 E4
Malvern Ct. RG1 33 G5
Manchester Rd. RG1 33 H3
Mandela Ct. RG1 33 F3
Mansfield Rd. RG1 32 C5
Maria Ct. RG30 32 A4
Market Pl,
  High St. RG1 32 D3
*Market Way,
  Buttermarket. RG1 32 D3
Marlborough Av. RG1 33 F6
Marlborough Ct. RG1 32 B5
Marquis Pl. RG1 33 G4
Marsh Ct. RG30 32 A3

Mason Ct. RG1 32 B3
Mason St. RG1 32 B3
Meadow Rd. RG1 32 C2
Mellor Walk. RG2 33 E5
Merchants Pl. RG1 32 D3
Milford Rd. RG1 32 C2
Mill Grn. RG4 33 F1
Mill La. RG1 32 D4
Mill Rd. RG4 33 E1
Millers Ct. RG4 33 F1
Milman Rd. RG2 33 E6
Minster St. RG1 32 D3
Mitcham Clo. RG2 33 E6
Monkley Ct. RG4 33 F1
Monks Way. RG30 32 A6
Montague St,
  Caversham. RG4 33 E1
Montague St,
  Reading. RG1 33 F4
Morgan Rd. RG1 33 E5
Mount Pleasant. RG1 33 E4
Mount Pleasant Gro.
  RG1 33 E5
Mount St. RG2 32 D5
Muirfield Clo. RG1 33 F4
Mundesley St. RG1 32 D4
Napier Rd. RG1 33 E2
Nelson Rd. RG4 33 E1
New Bright St. RG1 32 D4
New Rd. RG1 33 F5
Newark St. RG1 33 E4
Newport Rd. RG1 32 C1
Nimrod Way. RG2 32 D6
Norman Pl. RG1 32 D4
North Lodge Mws. RG1 32 A6
North St. RG1 32 D3
Northcourt Av. RG2 33 F6
Northfield Cotts. RG1 32 D2
Northfield Rd. RG1 32 D2
Northumberland Av.
  RG2 33 E6
Norton Rd. RG1 33 G3
Norwood Rd. RG1 33 G3
Oaklands. RG1 33 H4
Orchard St. RG1 32 D4
Ormsby St. RG1 32 B3
Orts Rd. RG1 33 F3
Osterley Ct. RG1 33 G4
Oxford Rd. RG1 32 A3
Paddock Rd. RG4 33 F1
Parkhouse La. RG30 32 A4
Parkside Rd. RG30 32 A4
Parthia Clo. RG1 32 D4
Patriot Pl. RG1 33 F3
Pelham Ct. RG30 32 A4
Pell St. RG1 32 D5
Pennyroyal Ct. RG1 32 C5
Petworth Ct. RG1 32 B4
Phoebe Ct. RG1 32 D4
Piggotts Rd. RG4 33 E1
Portman Rd. RG30 32 A2
Portway Clo. RG1 32 B5
Preston Rd. RG1 32 D6
Prince of Wales Av.
  RG30 32 A3
Princes St. RG1 33 F3
Promenade Rd. RG4 32 D1
Prospect St. RG1 32 B4
Queen Victoria St. RG1 32 D3
Queens Cotts. RG1 33 E3
Queens Lawn. RG1 33 G5
Queens Rd,
  Caversham. RG4 33 E1
Queens Rd,
  Reading. RG1 33 E3
*Queens Walk,
  Broad St Mall. RG1 32 D3
Radstock Rd. RG1 33 G3
Randolph Rd. RG1 32 C1
Reading Bri. RG1 33 E2
Redlands Rd. RG1 33 F4
Redlane Ct. RG1 33 F5
*Regent Ct,
  Gt Knollys St. RG1 32 D2
Regent St. RG1 33 F3
Regents Riverside. RG1 32 D1
Rembrandt Way. RG1 32 D1
Richfield Av. RG1 32 B1
River Rd. RG1 32 D1
Riversdale Ct. RG1 33 G3
Riverside Ct. RG1 33 E2
Rose Kiln La. RG1 32 D5
Rose Walk. RG1 32 D4
Ross Rd. RG1 32 C2
Rowley Rd. RG2 32 E6

Rupert Sq. RG1 33 G3
Rupert St. RG1 33 G3
Russell St. RG1 32 C4
Rutland Rd. RG30 32 A4
Sackville St. RG1 32 C4
St Andrews Ct. RG1 33 G4
St Bartholomews Rd.
  RG1 33 H3
St Giles Clo. RG1 33 E4
St Johns Hill. RG1 33 F3
St Johns Rd. RG1 33 F4
St Johns St. RG1 33 F3
St Marys Butts. RG1 32 D3
St Pauls Ct. RG1 32 D5
St Saviours Rd. RG1 32 C5
St Saviours Ter. RG1 32 C5
St Stephens Clo. RG4 32 D1
Salisbury Rd. RG30 32 B2
Sarum Ct. RG30 32 A4
School La. RG4 32 D1
School Ter. RG1 33 G3
Send Rd. RG4 33 F1
Shaw Rd. RG1 32 C5
Shenstone Rd. RG2 33 E6
Sherfield Dri. RG2 33 F6
Sherman Pl. RG1 32 D4
Sherman Rd. RG1 32 D4
Shinfield Rd. RG2 33 F6
Short St. RG1 33 E5
Sidmouth St. RG1 33 E4
Silver St. RG1 33 E4
Simmonds St. RG1 32 D4
Somerstown Ct. RG1 32 B4
South St. RG1 33 E4
Southampton St. RG1 32 D4
Southcote Farm La.
  RG30 32 A6
Southcote La. RG30 32 A5
Southcote Rd. RG30 32 A5
Southern Hill. RG1 33 F5
Spring Gro. RG1 33 E5
Spring Ter. RG2 33 E5
Stanley Gro. RG2 32 B3
Stanley St. RG1 32 B3
Stanshawe Rd. RG1 32 D2
Star Rd. RG4 33 F1
Station App. RG1 32 D2
Station Hill. RG1 32 D2
Station Rd. RG1 32 D3
Sun St. RG1 33 G3
Surrey Rd. RG2 33 E6
Sutherlands Av. RG1 33 F5
Sutton Walk. RG1 33 F5
Suttons Park Av. RG6 33 H2
Swainstone Rd. RG2 33 E6
Swallows Ct. RG1 32 A6
Swan Pl. RG1 32 D4
Swansea Rd. RG1 32 C2
Talbot Ct. RG1 32 D4
Tallis La. RG30 32 A6
Taylor Ct. RG1 32 B4
Tazewell Ct. RG1 32 B4
Temple Pl. RG1 32 D4
Tessa Rd. RG1 32 C1
Tetbury Ct. RG1 32 B4
Thames Av. RG1 32 D1
Thames Side. RG1 32 D1
Thames Side Prom.
  RG1 32 C1
The Brookmill. RG1 32 B6
The Causeway. RG4 33 F1
The Chancellors Way.
  RG6 33 G6
The Dell. RG1 33 E4
The Firs. RG1 32 C4
The Forbury. RG1 33 E3
The Grove. RG1 33 E4
The Mews. RG1 33 H4
The Mount. RG1 33 F5
The Old La. RG1 32 B5
The Parade. RG30 32 A6
The Queens Dri. RG6 33 G6
The Willows. RG4 32 D1
*Thorn La,
  Duke St. RG1 33 E3
Thorn St. RG1 32 C3
Tilehurst Rd. RG1 32 C4
Tintern Cres. RG1 32 C5
Tippett Rise. RG2 32 D5
Town Pl. RG1 33 F4
Trafalgar Ct. RG30 32 A4
Trafford Rd. RG1 32 B2
Trelleck Rd. RG1 32 C6

Treyarnon Ct. RG1 33 G4
Trinity Pl. RG1 32 C3
Troon Ct. RG1 33 F4
Tudor Rd. RG1 32 D2
Tupsley Rd. RG1 32 C6
Tyberton Pl. RG1 32 C6
Union St. RG1 32 D3
Upavon Dri. RG1 32 B5
Upper Crown St. RG1 33 E5
Upper Redlands Rd.
RG1 33 F5
Vachel Rd. RG1 32 D3
Valentia Clot. RG30 32 A2
Valentia Rd. RG30 32 A3
Valerie Ct. RG1 32 B5
Valpy St. RG1 32 D2
Vanbrugh Ct. RG1 33 G4
Vastern Rd. RG1 32 D2
Vicarage Rd. RG2 33 E6
Victoria Sq. RG1 33 F3
Victoria St. RG1 33 F4
Victoria Way. RG1 33 G3
Waldeck St. RG1 33 E5
Warwick Rd. RG2 33 E6
Waterloo Rise. RG2 33 E6
Waterloo Rd. RG2 32 D5
Waterman Pl. RG1 32 D1
Waterside Gdns. RG1 32 D4
Watlington St. RG1 33 E3
Waybrook Cres. RG1 33 H5
Waylen St. RG1 32 C3
Weighbridge Rd. RG1 32 C2
Weirside Ct. RG1 33 F3
Weldale Pl. RG1 32 D2
Weldale St. RG1 32 D2
Wensley Rd. RG1 32 A6
West Fryerne. RG30 32 A4
West Hill. RG1 32 D4
West St. RG1 32 D4
Westcote Rd. RG30 32 A4
Western Elms Av.
RG30 32 A4
Western Rd. RG1 32 B4
Whitby Dri. RG1 33 F5
Whiteknights Rd. RG6 33 H5
Whitley Park La. RG2 33 H6
Whitley St. RG2 33 E5
William St. RG1 32 C3
Wilton Rd. RG30 32 A3
Windsor Sq. RG1 33 E4
Winser Dri. RG30 32 A6
Wiston Ter. RG1 32 A6
Wokingham Rd. RG6 33 H4
Wolseley St. RG1 32 C5
Wolsey Rd. RG4 32 D1
Wood Green Clo. RG30 32 B3
Woodstock St. RG1 33 G3
Yew La. RG1 32 B6
Yield Hall Pl. RG1 32 D3
York Rd. RG1 32 C2
Zinzan St. RG1 32 C3

SANDHURST

Abingdon Rd. GU47 35 E3
Acacia Av. GU47 35 E3
Ackrells Mead. GU47 34 A3
Albion Rd. GU47 34 D4
Allenby Rd. GU47 35 H6
Allendale Clo. GU47 34 B2
Alton Ride. GU17 34 D6
Ambarrow Cres. GU47 34 B3
Ambarrow La. GU47 34 A2
Andover Pl. GU17 34 D6
Apple Tree Way. GU47 35 E3
Atrebatti Rd. GU47 35 E3
Avocet Cres. GU47 35 F4
Bacon Clo. GU47 35 E6
Balintore Ct. GU47 35 E5
Balliol Way. GU47 35 F3
Barkis Mead. GU47 35 F2
Beaulieu Gdns. GU17 34 D6
Beech Ride. GU47 34 D3
Beechnut Dri. GU17 34 D6
Bernersh Clo. GU47 35 E3
Berrybank. GU47 35 F6
Birdwood Rd. GU47 35 H5
Birkbeck Pl. GU47 35 F3
Bittern Clo. GU47 35 F4
Blackbird Clo. GU47 35 F4
Blackcap Pl. GU47 35 F4
Bluethroat Clo. GU47 34 D5

Branksome Hill Rd.
GU47 35 F5
Braye Clo. GU47 35 E3
Breach La. GU47 34 C4
Brittain Ct. GU47 34 D5
Brook Clo. GU47 35 F3
Brookside. GU47 34 D5
Broomacres. GU47 34 C4
Bullfinch Clo. GU47 35 F4
Burghead Clo. GU47 35 F5
Burley Way. GU47 35 E6
Burne-Jones Dri. GU47 35 F6
Byron Dri. RG45 34 C1
Cambridge Rd. GU47 35 F3
Campbell Clo. GU46 34 A6
Cannon Clo. GU47 35 G4
Capper Rd. GU47 35 H5
Carrick La. GU46 34 A6
Castlecraig Ct. GU47 35 E5
Cavendish Pk. GU47 35 F6
Caves Farm Clo. GU47 34 B4
Cedars Clo. GU47 34 B4
Centurion Clo. GU47 35 E4
Chaffinch Clo. GU47 35 F4
Chapel Square. GU47 35 G6
Charlton Ct. GU47 35 F3
Chelwood Dri. GU47 34 B3
Cherry Tree Clo. GU47 35 E3
Cheviot Rd. GU47 34 B3
Chiltern Rd. GU47 34 B2
Christchurch La. GU17 34 D6
Church Rd,
Owlsmoor. GU47 35 F3
Church Rd,
Sandhurst. GU47 34 B3
Clarke Cres. GU47 35 G5
Coachmans Gro. GU47 34 D5
Cock-A-Dobby. GU47 34 C3
College Cres. GU47 35 G4
College Rd. GU47 35 F5
Compton Clo. GU47 34 D3
Connaught Clo. GU47 34 B1
Constable Way. GU47 35 F6
Cookham Clo. GU47 34 D3
Copperfield Rd. GU47 35 F2
Cormorant Clo. GU47 35 F4
Cornbunting Clo. GU47 35 F4
Cotswold Rd. GU47 34 B3
Cox Grn. GU47 35 E6
Crake Pl. GU47 35 F4
Crane Ct. GU47 35 F4
Cricket Hill Rd. GU46 34 A6
Crofters Clo. GU47 34 C4
Crown Pl. GU47 35 F3
Crowthorne Rd. GU47 34 C4
Cruikshank Lea. GU47 35 F6
Culver Rd. GU47 34 C4
Dale Gdns. GU47 34 C4
Dalley Ct. GU47 35 F5
Darby Green La. GU17 34 C6
Darleydale Clo. GU47 35 F2
Davis Gdns. GU47 35 F5
Devon Clo. GU47 35 E5
Dovedale Clo. GU47 35 F2
Durham Rd. GU47 35 F2
Eagles Nest. GU47 34 B3
Edgbarrow Rise. GU47 34 C2
Egerton Rd. GU47 35 G6
Evenlode Way. GU47 35 E4
Evesham Walk. GU47 35 E3
Fairmead Clo. GU47 35 F5
Fakenham Way. GU47 35 E3
Faringdon Clo. GU47 34 D4
Farncrosse Clo. GU47 34 D4
Faversham Rd. GU47 35 E3
Ferryhill Dri. GU47 34 B3
Fielding Rd. GU47 35 F5
Findhorn Clo. GU47 35 F5
Firtree Clo. GU47 34 B4
Florence Rd. GU47 35 F5
Forbes Chase. GU47 35 E5
Forest End Rd. GU47 34 B3
Foresters Way. GU47 35 G1
Fortrose Clo. GU47 35 F5
Fraser Mead. GU47 35 F6
Frodsham Way. GU47 35 F4
Frys La. GU46 34 A5
Georgeham Rd. GU47 35 F6
Gibbons Clo. GU47 35 D4
Girton Clo. GU47 35 G3
Glen Innes. GU47 35 G3
Godfrey Clo. GU47 35 E4
Gordon Walk. GU46 34 A6
Gothic Ct. GU47 34 D5

Goughs Mdw. GU47 34 C5
Governors Rd. GU47 35 G6
Gower Park. GU47 35 E5
Grampian Rd. GU47 34 B2
Grantham Clo. GU47 35 F3
Green La. GU47 34 D4
Greenways. GU47 34 C3
Grove Cres. GU47 35 G6
Haig Rd. GU47 35 G6
Hailsham Clo. GU47 35 E3
Hallmark Clo. GU47 35 F4
Hancombe Rd. GU47 34 B2
Hartley Clo. GU17 34 D6
Hartsleap Clo. GU47 34 C3
Hartsleap Rd. GU47 34 C4
Harvard Rd. GU47 35 G3
Hatherwood. GU46 34 A6
Haydon Pl. GU46 34 A6
Hearsey Gdns. GU17 34 D6
Hepworth Croft. GU47 35 F6
Hexham Clo. GU47 35 E2
High St,
Little Sandhurst. GU47 34 B3
High St,
Sandhurst. GU47 35 G5
Hillside. GU47 35 G5
Hogarth Clo. GU47 35 F6
Hone Hill. GU47 34 C4
Hopeman Clo. GU47 35 E4
Hormer Clo. GU47 35 F3
Hornbeam Clo. GU47 35 E3
Horsham Rd. GU47 35 E3
Humber Way. GU47 35 E4
Hungerford Clo. GU47 34 D4
Inverness Way. GU47 35 E5
Isis Way. GU47 35 E4
Jacob Rd. GU47 35 H5
Jennys Walk. GU46 34 A6
Keble Way. GU47 35 G2
Kevins Dri. GU46 34 A5
Keynsham Way. GU47 35 E2
Kilmuir Clo. GU47 35 E5
Kings Keep. GU47 34 D3
Kings Walk. GU47 35 G6
Kingsley Clo. RG45 34 D1
Kirkham Clo. GU47 35 E2
Lamborne Clo. GU47 34 B3
Landseer Clo. GU47 35 F6
Larkswood Clo. GU47 34 C3
Laundry La. GU47 35 F6
Lewisham Way. GU47 35 E2
Little Moor. GU47 34 D3
Lodge Gro. GU46 34 A6
Long Mickle. GU47 34 C3
Longdown Rd. GU47 34 C3
Lower Church Rd.
GU47 34 A3
Lowry Clo. GU47 35 F6
Lych Gate Clo. GU47 34 A4
Lyndhurst Av. GU17 34 D6
Madox Brown End.
GU47 35 F6
Magdalene Rd. GU47 35 G2
Magnolia Clo. GU47 35 E3
Maple Clo. GU47 34 B3
Marshall Rd. GU47 35 F2
Masefield Gdns. RG45 34 C1
Mason Pl. GU47 34 B4
Maxine Clo. GU47 34 C3
May Clo. GU47 35 F4
Maybrick Clo. GU47 34 A3
Melksham Clo. GU47 35 E2
Merton Clo. GU47 34 C3
Mickle Hill. GU47 34 C3
Millins Clo. GU47 35 F3
Moffatts Clo. GU47 34 C4
Montgomery Clo.
GU47 34 D4
Moor Clo. GU47 35 F3
Moray Av. GU47 35 E4
Mordaunt Rd. RG45 34 C1
Mount Pleasant. GU47 34 B2
Mountbatten Clo. GU47 34 B3
Mulberry Clo. GU47 35 E3
Munnings Dri. GU47 35 F6
New Rd. GU47 34 B4
New Town Rd. GU47 34 C4
Nightingale Gdns.
GU47 34 C4
Nuffield Clo. GU47 35 G3
Oak Av. GU47 35 E3
Oaktree Way. GU47 34 C3
Okingham Clo. GU47 35 E3
Old Forge End. GU47 34 D5

Orchard Gate. GU47 34 D4
Owlsmoor Rd. GU47 35 E4
Oxford Rd. GU47 35 F2
Park Dri. GU46 34 A6
Park Rd. GU47 34 D5
Parsons Field. GU47 34 D4
Peddlars Gro. GU46 34 A6
Peggotty Pl. GU47 35 F2
Peterouse Clo. GU47 35 G2
Pine Clo. GU47 35 G5
Pinehill Rise. GU47 34 D4
Pinehill Rd. RG45 35 E1
Pinewood Clo. GU47 34 B4
Pond Croft. GU46 34 A6
Potley Hill. GU46 34 A6
Primrose Way. GU47 34 D3
Prince Dri. GU47 34 B3
Rackstraw Rd. GU47 35 E3
Raeburn Way. GU47 35 E6
Range Ride. GU47 35 G5
Range Vw. GU47 35 G4
Rawlinson Rd. GU47 35 H6
Reading Rd. GU46 34 A6
Rectory Clo. GU47 34 B4
Regents Pl. GU47 34 D4
Reynolds Grn. GU47 35 E6
Richmond Rd. GU47 35 F4
Ringwood Rd. GU17 34 D6
Ripplesmore Clo. GU47 34 C4
Roberts Rd. GU47 35 H6
Robin La. GU47 35 E4
Rockfield Way. GU47 35 E4
Romsey Clo. GU177 35 E6
Rookwood Av. GU47 35 F2
Rosedene La. GU47 35 E4
Rosemary La. GU17 34 D6
Rother Clo. GU47 35 E4
Royal Oak Clo. GU46 34 A6
Rugby Clo. GU47 35 F3
Ryan Mt. GU47 34 B4
Saddler Cnr. GU47 34 D5
St Georges Ct. GU47 34 B4
St Helens Cres. GU47 34 C4
St Helens Dri. GU47 34 C4
St Johns Rd. GGU17 34 D5
St Marys Clo. GU47 34 C4
St Michaels Rd. GU47 34 B4
Sandhurst La. GU17 34 D4
Sandhurst Rd. RG45 34 D1
Sandhurst Rd,
Yateley. GU46 34 A6
Sandy La. GU47 34 B3
School Hill. GU47 34 B3
Scotland Hill. GU47 34 C4
Seebys Oak. GU47 35 F6
Selbourne Clo. GU17 35 E6
Severn Clo. GU47 35 E4
Shrivenham Clo. GU47 35 E4
Silver Hill. GU47 34 D5
Somerville Cres. GU46 34 A6
Sonninge Clo. GU47 34 C4
South Meadow. RG45 35 F1
South Rd. RG45 35 F1
Southampton Clo. GU17 35 E6
Spring Woods. GU47 34 D3
Squirrel Clo. GU47 34 C4
Steerforth Copse. GU47 35 F2
Sterling Gdns. GU47 35 F4
Stubbs Folly. GU47 35 E5
Sun Ray Est. GU47 34 B4
Swan La. GU47 34 C5
Sycamore Clo. GU47 34 C4
Sylvan Ridge. GU47 34 C3
Tarbat Ct. GU47 35 E4
Templar Clo. GU47 34 B4
The Breech. GU47 35 F5
The Broadway. GU47 34 D5
The Close. GU47 34 D5
Theal Clo. GU47 34 D4
Thibet Rd. GU47 34 D4
Thorburn Chase. GU47 35 E3
Tottenham Walk. GU47 35 E3
Travis La. GU47 34 D5
Trinity. GU47 34 D4
Trotwood Clo. GU47 35 F2
Turner Pl. GU47 35 F6
Union Clo. GU47 35 F2
Uplands Clo. GU47 34 C4
Valley Vw. GU47 34 B4
Victoria Rd. GU47 35 F3
Vulcan Clo. GU47 34 C5
Vulcan Way. GU47 34 C5
Wadham. GU47 35 G3
Waltham Rd. GU47 35 E3

Wantage Rd. GU47 35 E4
Wargrove Dri. GU47 35 E4
Warren Clo. GU47 34 C4
Wasdale Clo. GU47 35 E2
Waterhouse Mead.
GU47 35 E5
Weaver Moss. GU47 34 D5
Wellburn Clo. GU47 34 D5
Wellington Clo. GU47 35 E4
Wellington Rd. GU47 34 D4
Wellington Ter. GU47 35 F5
Westbourne Rd. GU47 35 F5
Weybridge Mead. GU46 34 A5
Whistler Gro. GU47 35 E6
White Rd. GU47 35 G6
Whitmore Clo. GU47 35 E3
Whittle Clo. GU47 34 B3
Willow Way. GU47 34 B3
Willows End. GU47 34 C4
Winchester Way. GU17 34 D6
Windrush Heights.
GU47 34 C4
Windsor Ride. GU47 35 H5
Wokingham Rd. GU47 34 A1
Woodbine Clo. GU47 34 D5
Woodlands Ct. GU47 35 G3
Woodside. GU47 35 G5
Yale Clo. GU47 35 G2
Yateley Rd. GU47 34 A4
Yeovil Rd. GU47 35 F3
York Town Rd. GU47 34 C5
York Way. GU47 34 C4
Zenith Clo. GU47 35 F3

SHINFIELD

Arborfield Rd. RG2 42 D3
Babbington Rd. RG2 42 B1
Brookers Hill. RG2 42 A3
Burlingham Clo. RG2 42 D3
Chestnut Cres. RG2 42 D3
Church La. RG2 42 B1
Cutbush La. RG2 42 C1
Drewett Clo. RG2 42 B1
Fairmead Rd. RG2 42 D2
Farmers Clo. RG2 42 A1
Goddard Clo. RG2 42 D2
Harness Clo. RG2 42 A1
Hirtes Av. RG2 42 C1
Hollow La. RG2 42 C1
Hyde End La. RG7 42 A3
Hyde End Rd. RG2 42 A1
Ilbury Clo. RG2 42 C2
Kendal Av. RG2 42 D1
Lane End Clo. RG2 42 C1
Leyland Gdns. RG2 42 C1
Longmore Rd. RG2 42 A1
Lexington Gro. RG2 42 A1
Millworth La. RG2 42 D3
Milsom Clo. RG2 42 C2
Mylum Clo. RG2 42 B1
Oatlands Rd. RG2 42 D2
Old Whitley Wood La.
RG2 42 B1
Pattinson Rd. RG2 42 B1
Pendred Rd. RG2 42 C1
Rosecroft Way. RG2 42 C1
Salmond Rd. RG2 42 B1
Sampage Clo. RG2 42 A1
Sandleford Clo. RG2 42 D3
School Grn. RG2 42 D3
Seymour Av. RG2 42 D3
Shinfield Rd. RG2 42 D2
Swallowfield Dri. RG2 42 A1
The Manor. RG2 42 C2
The Maying. RG2 42 C2
Vicarage Ct. RG2 42 C2
Vickers Clo. RG2 42 D3
Village Clo. RG2 42 A1
Wheatfields Rd. RG2 42 D2
Whitley Wood La. RG2 42 A1
Woodman Clo. RG2 42 A1
Wychelm Rd. RG2 42 D2

SLOUGH

Adelphi Gdns. SL1 36 B4
Alan Way. SL3 37 H2
Albert Clo. SL1 36 D5
Albert St. SL1 36 C5

Albion Clo. SL1	36 D4
Aldborough Spur. SL1	36 B2
Aldin Av N. SL1	37 E4
Aldin Av S. SL1	37 E5
Alexandra Rd. SL1	36 B5
Almons Way. SL2	37 E1
Alpha St. SL1	36 D5
Amanda Ct. SL3	37 G5
Appletree La. SL3	37 F5
Arborfield Clo. SL1	36 C5
Arthur Rd. SL1	36 B4
Arundel Ct. SL3	37 G6
August End. SL3	37 H1
Australia Rd. SL1	37 E4
Aylesbury Cres. SL1	36 B2
Azalea Way.SL3	37 H2
Bannister Clo. SL3	37 H5
Bath Rd. SL1	36 A4
Baxter Clo. SL1	36 C5
Baylis Rd. SL1	36 B3
*Beauchamp Ct, Pool La. SL1	36 B3
Beech Rd. SL3	37 H5
Beechwood Gdns. SL1	36 C5
Belfast Av. SL1	36 A2
Belgrave Pl. SL1	37 E5
Belgrave Rd. SL1	36 C3
Bell Clo. SL2	37 F1
Bellvue Pl. SL1	36 D6
Benson Clo. SL2	36 D3
Beresford Av. SL2	37 F3
Berryfield. SL2	37 F2
Beverley Ct. SL1	37 E5
Birley Rd. SL1	36 B2
Bishops Rd. SL1	36 D5
Blackthorn Dell. SL3	37 F5
Blair Rd. SL1	36 B4
Blandford Clo. SL3	37 G5
Blandford Ct. SL3	37 G6
Blandford Rd N. SL3	37 G5
Blandford Rd S. SL3	37 G6
Blinco La. SL3	37 H1
Borderside. SL2	37 E2
Boston Gro. SL1	36 A1
Botham Dri. SL1	36 B5
Bourne Rd. SL1	36 A5
Brackenforde. SL3	37 F5
Bradley Rd. SL1	36 B3
Brammas Clo. SL1	36 A5
Bristol Way. SL2	36 C4
Broad Platts. SL3	37 G6
Broadmark Rd. SL2	37 E3
Brunel Way. SL1	36 C4
Bryant Av. SL2	36 C1
Buckingham Av E. SL1	36 A2
Buckingham Gdns. SL1	36 C5
Buckland Av. SL3	37 E6
Bulstrode Pl. SL1	36 C6
Burlington Av. SL1	36 C5
Canada Rd. SL1	37 E4
Carlisle Rd. SL1	36 A3
Carlton Rd. SL2	37 E3
Carmarthen Rd. SL1	36 B3
Carrington Rd. SL1	36 C3
Castle St.SL1	36 D6
Chalvey Gdns. SL1	36 C5
Chalvey Pk. SL1	36 C5
Chalvey Rd E. SL1	36 B5
Chalvey Rd W. SL1	36 B5
Chapel St. SL1	36 D5
Charles Gdns. SL2	37 E2
Cherry Av. SL3	37 G5
Chester Rd. SL1	36 B1
Chestnut Av. SL3	37 H5
Chichester Ct. SL1	37 E5
Church La. SL2	37 F1
Church St. SL1	36 C5
Church St, Chalvey. SL1	36 A5
Churchfield Mews. SL2	37 E1
Cippenham La. SL1	36 A4
Clements Clo. SL1	37 E5
Clifton Rd. SL1	37 E5
Clive Ct. SL1	36 A5
Cockett Rd. SL3	37 H5
Coftards. SL2	37 G2
College Av. SL1	36 B5
Colonial Rd. SL1	37 E4
Concorde Way. SL1	36 A5
Conegar Ct. SL1	36 B4
Connaught Rd. SL1	37 E4
Coronation Av. SL3	37 H1
Court Cres. SL1	36 B1
Cranbourne Rd. SL1	36 A4
Cromwell Dri. SL1	36 C1
Damson Gro. SL1	36 A5
Dandridge Clo. SL3	37 G6
Darvills La. SL1	36 B5
Dashwood Clo. SL3	37 F6
Datchet Rd. SL3	36 D6
Dawes Moor Clo. SL2	37 G2
Devon Av. SL1	36 A1
Diamond Rd. SL1	37 E4
Diana Clo. SL3	37 H2
Dolphin Rd. SL1	37 E4
Dornels. SL2	37 F2
Downs Rd. SL3	37 G5
Dudley Ct. SL1	36 D6
Dunbar Clo. SL2	37 E2
Eastfield Clo. SL1	36 D5
Edmunds Way. SL2	37 F1
Elliman Av. SL2	36 C2
Ellis Av. SL1	36 B4
Elmwood Rd. SL2	37 E3
Ely Av. SL1	36 A1
Emerald Ct. SL1	36 C5
Everard Av. SL1	36 B4
Farm Cres. SL2	37 F1
Farm La. SL1	36 B2
Farnham Rd. SL1	36 A1
Fielding Gdns. SL3	37 F5
First Cres. SL1	36 A1
Fishguard Spur. SL1	37 E5
Fleetwood Rd. SL2	36 D3
Fox Rd. SL3	37 G6
Foxherne. SL3	37 F5
Frank Suttton Way. SL1	36 A3
*Fraunchies Ct, Pool La. SL1	36 B3
Galloway Chase. SL2	36 D3
Gatewick Clo. SL1	36 C4
George Green Rd. SL3	37 H2
Gilliat Rd. SL1	36 C3
Gilmore Clo. SL3	37 F4
Glanmor Rd. SL2	37 F3
Glenavon Gdns. SL3	37 G6
Glentworth Pl. SL1	36 A4
Gloucester Av. SL1	36 A1
Godolphin Rd. SL1	36 B2
Goodman Pk. SL2	37 F4
Gosling Grn. SL3	37 H6
Gosling Rd. SL3	37 H5
Grace Ct. SL1	36 A3
Grafton Clo. SL3	37 H2
Grangewood. SL3	37 F1
Grant Av. SL1	36 C2
Granville Av. SL2	36 A1
Grasmere Av. SL2	36 D3
Grays Pl. SL2	36 D3
Grays Rd. SL1	36 C3
Greendale Mews. SL2	36 D3
Grove Clo. SL1	36 D5
Hadlow Ct. SL1	36 A3
Halking Croft. SL3	37 F5
Hampshire Av. SL1	36 A1
Hanover Clo. SL1	36 D6
Harewood Pl. SL1	37 E5
Harris Gdns. SL1	36 A4
Hartland Clo. SL1	36 B4
Hatfield Rd. SL1	36 D5
Hawthorne Cres. SL1	36 C2
Hawtrey Clo. SL1	37 F5
Hazlemere Rd. SL2	37 E3
Hempson Av. SL3	37 F5
Hencroft St. SL1	36 D5
Henry Rd. SL1	36 B4
Hermitage Clo. SL3	37 F5
Herschel St. SL1	36 C5
High St. SL1	37 D5
High St, Chalvey. SL1	36 A5
Hillary Rd. SL3	37 H5
Hillersdon. SL2	37 E1
Hillside. SL1	36 B5
Hilperton Rd. SL1	36 C4
Holmedale. SL2	37 F2
Homewood. SL3	37 G2
Hornbeam Gdns. SL1	36 D6
Hubert Rd. SL3	37 H6
Hughendon Rd. SL1	36 B2
Hurworth Rd. SL1	37 F6
India Rd. SL2	37 E4
INDUSTRIAL & RETAIL:	
The Business Centre. SL2	37 E3
John Taylor Ct. SL1	36 A4
Juniper Ct. SL1	37 E5
Kaywood Clo. SL3	37 G6
Keel Dri. SL1	36 A5
Kendal Clo. SL2	36 D3
Kendal Dri. SL2	36 D3
Kendrick Rd. SL3	37 F6
Kenilworth Clo. SL1	36 D6
Keswick Ct. SL2	36 D3
King Edward St. SL1	36 B5
Kings Rd. SL1	36 B6
Kirkwall Spur. SL1	36 B1
Knolton Way. SL2	37 E1
La Roche Clo. SL3	37 F5
Ladbrooke Rd. SL1	36 A5
Ladyday Pl. SL1	36 A4
Lake Av. SL1	36 A3
Lambert Av. SL3	37 H5
Langley Rd. SL3	37 F5
Lansdowne Av. SL1	36 B4
Lansdowne Ct. SL1	36 C4
Lascelles Rd. SL3	37 E6
Laurel Av. SL3	37 H5
Ledgers Rd. SL1	36 B5
Leeds Rd. SL1	36 B3
Leiston Spur. SL1	36 B1
Leith Clo. SL1	36 D4
Lerwick Dri. SL1	36 B1
Lismore Park. SL2	36 C2
Litcham Spur. SL1	36 B2
Littledown Rd. SL1	36 C3
Littleport Spur. SL1	36 B2
Locke Gdns. SL3	37 F5
Loddon Spur. SL1	36 B2
London Rd. SL3	37 E5
Lynwood Av. SL3	37 G6
Mackenzie St. SL1	36 C4
Magnolia Gdns. SL3	37 F6
Malpas Rd. SL2	37 E3
Mansell Clo. SL2	37 E1
Maple Cres. SL2	37 F3
Martin Rd. SL1	36 B5
Maryside. SL3	37 H5
Meadow Rd. SL3	37 H6
Melbourne Av. SL1	36 A2
Mere Rd. SL1	36 D6
Merton Ct. SL1	36 D5
Merton Rd. SL1	36 D5
Middle Green. SL3	37 H3
Middlegreen Rd. SL3	37 G5
Mildenhall Rd. SL1	36 B2
Mill St. SL2	36 D3
Mina Av. SL3	37 G5
Mirador Cres. SL2	37 E2
Moat Dri. SL2	37 F1
Montague Rd. SL1	36 C3
Montem La. SL1	36 A4
Montgomery Pl. SL2	37 F2
Moray Dri. SL2	37 E2
Moreau Walk. SL3	37 H2
Mortimer Rd. SL3	37 H6
Mountbatten Clo. SL1	36 D5
Muddy La. SL1	36 C1
Mundesley Spur. SL1	36 B2
Myrtle Cres. SL2	36 D2
New Sq. SL1	36 C4
Newberry Way. SL1	36 B5
Newnham Clo. SL2	36 D3
Nixey Clo. SL1	37 E5
Norfolk Av. SL1	36 A1
North Green. SL1	36 C3
Northampton Av. SL1	36 A1
Norway Dri. SL2	37 E1
Nursery La. SL3	37 G4
Oakley Cres. SL1	36 B2
Oatlands Dri. SL1	36 A1
Oban Ct. SL1	36 B4
Osborne St. SL1	36 C5
Palmerston Av. SL3	37 F5
Park La. SL3	37 E6
Park St. SL1	36 D5
Paxton Av. SL1	36 A5
Petersfield Av. SL2	37 D3
Pitts Rd. SL1	36 A3
Plough Lees La. SL1	36 C3
Pool La. SL1	36 B3
Post Office La. SL3	37 G2
Preston Rd. SL2	37 F3
Prestwood. SL2	37 E2
Princes St. SL1	37 E4
Priors Clo. SL1	36 D5
Quaves Rd. SL3	37 F5
Queens Ct. SL1	36 D3
Queens Rd. SL1	36 C3
Queensmere Rd. SL1	36 D4
Quinbrooks. SL2	37 F2
Ragstone Rd. SL1	36 B5
Railway Ter. SL2	36 C4
Rambler La. SL3	37 G6
Randolph Rd. SL3	37 H6
Ravensfield. SL3	37 G4
Red Ct. SL1	36 B4
Redcott Ms. SL1	37 F6
Reddington Dri. SL3	37 H6
Redwood Gdns. SL1	36 A2
Regent Ct. SL1	36 C2
Richmond Cres. SL1	36 D4
Rixon Clo. SL3	37 H1
Rochfords Gdns. SL2	37 F3
Ronaldsay Spur. SL1	36 C1
Rossiter Clo. SL3	37 H6
Rutland Av. SL1	36 A1
St Bernards Rd. SL3	37 F6
St Johns Rd. SL2	36 D3
St Laurence Way. SL1	36 D5
St Marys Rd. SL3	37 H4
St Pauls Av. SL2	36 D3
Salt Hill Av. SL1	36 A4
Salt Hill Dri. SL1	36 A3
Salt Hill Way. SL1	36 A3
Second Cres. SL1	36 A1
Sermed Ct. SL2	37 F3
Seymour Rd. SL1	36 A4
Shackleton Rd. SL1	36 C3
Shaggy Calf La. SL2	37 D2
Sheehy Way. SL2	37 F2
Sheffield Rd. SL1	36 A2
Sherman Rd. SL1	36 C1
Sherwood Clo. SL3	37 H6
Shortfern. SL2	37 F2
Slough Rd. SL3	36 B6
Snape Spur. SL1	36 B1
South Green. SL1	36 C3
Spackmans Way. SL1	36 A6
Springate Field. SL3	37 H5
Stanley Cotts. SL2	36 C4
Starwood Ct. SL3	37 F5
Statfield Rd. SL2	36 D4
Stewart Av. SL1	36 C1
Stile Rd. SL3	37 G6
Stoke Gdns. SL1	36 C3
Stoke Poges La. SL1	36 B4
Stoke Rd. SL2	36 C4
Stokesay. SL2	36 D2
Stranraer Gdns. SL1	36 C4
Sumburgh Spur. SL1	36 B1
Sussex Clo. SL1	37 E5
Sussex Pl. SL1	37 E5
Sutton Av. SL3	37 F5
Sycamore Walk. SL3	37 H2
Sydney Gro. SL1	36 A2
The Cherries. SL2	37 F2
The Crescent. SL1	36 B5
The Drive. SL3	37 H5
The Frithe. SL2	37 E2
The Glen. SL3	37 F6
The Green. SL1	36 A5
The Grove. SL1	36 D5
The Link. SL2	37 F2
The Mews. SL1	36 C6
The Normans. SL2	37 E1
Third Cres. SL1	36 A1
Thurston Rd. SL1	36 B1
Trelawney Av. SL3	37 G6
Tuns La. SL1	36 A4
Turner Rd. SL3	37 F5
Turton Way. SL1	36 B5
Upton Clo. SL1	36 C6
Upton Court Rd. SL3	36 D6
Upton Pk. SL1	36 C5
Upton Rd. SL1	36 D6
Uxbridge Rd. SL1	37 E4
Vale Gro. SL1	36 C6
Vicarage Pl. SL1	37 E5
Victoria Rd. SL2	37 F4
Victoria St. SL1	36 D5
Wallis Clo. SL1	37 E5
Warren Clo. SL3	37 H6
Warrington Av. SL1	36 A1
Waterbeach Clo. SL1	36 B1
Waterbeach Rd. SL1	36 A1
Waverley Rd. SL1	36 A1
Webb Clo. SL3	37 H6
Welden. SL2	37 F2
Wellesley Rd. SL1	36 D4
Wellington St. SL1	36 C4
Westfield La. SL3	37 H2
Wexham Rd. SL1	37 E1
Wheatland Rd. SL3	37 F6
Whitby Rd. SL1	36 A2
White Clo. SL1	36 B3
White Hart Rd. SL1	36 A6
Whiteford Rd. SL2	36 C1
Whitehaven. SL1	36 D3
Whittenham Clo. SL2	37 D3
William St. SL1	36 C4
Windmill Rd. SL1	36 A4
Windsor Rd. SL1	36 C6
Winvale. SL1	36 C6
Winwood. SL2	37 F2
Withy Croft. SL3	37 H2
Woodland Av. SL1	36 B3
Worcester Gdns. SL1	36 B5
Yew Tree Rd. SL1	36 D6
York Av. SL1	36 A2

THATCHAM

Acorn Dri. RG18	39 E2
Adwood Ct. RG19	39 F4
Agricola Way. RG19	39 F5
Alexander Rd. RG19	39 F5
Almond Dri. RG19	39 E3
Alston Ms. RG19	38 D5
Anvil Ct. RG19	39 F4
Appelford Clo. RG19	39 F5
Archange Way. RG18	39 G3
Arkle Way. RG19	38 A4
Arrowsmith Way. RG19	39 G5
Ash Gate. RG18	39 G3
Ashbourne Way. RG19	38 C4
Ashman Rd. RG19	39 G5
Ashmore Green Rd. RG18	38 C1
Ashworth Dri. RG19	38 D5
Aylesford Way. RG19	39 G5
Baily Av. RG18	38 C3
Barfield Rd. RG18	38 C3
Barley Clo. RG19	39 G5
Barley Ct. RG19	39 G5
Bath Rd. RG18	38 B3
Bath Rd. RG18	39 F4
Beancroft Rd. RG19	39 E5
Beech Walk. RG19	39 F5
Benham Hill. RG18	38 A3
Berkshire Dri. RG19	39 H5
Betteridge Rd. RG19	39 G5
Beverley Clo. RG18	38 D2
Billington Way. RG18	38 D2
Blackdown Way. RG19	38 D5
Blackthorn Dri. RG18	39 E2
Bluebell Way. RG18	39 E2
Bluecoats. RG18	39 E3
Blythe Rd. RG19	39 F5
Bodmin Clo. RG19	38 D5
Bollingbroke Way. RG19	39 G4
Boscowen Way. RG19	39 G5
Botany Clo. RG19	39 G4
Bourne Arch. RG18	38 C3
Bourne Rd. RG19	38 C3
Bowes Rd. RG19	39 E5
Bowling Green Rd. RG18	38 B2
Bradley-Moore Sq. RG18	39 F3
Braemore Clo. RG19	39 E5
Bramwell Clo. RG19	39 G5
Brent Clo. RG19	39 E5
Broadmeadow End. RG18	39 G3
Broadway. RG19	39 E4
Brooks Rd. RG18	39 F3
Brownfield Rd. RG18	38 D4
Browning Clo. RG18	38 D3
Buchanan Sq. RG19	39 F6
Burns Walk. RG18	38 D3
Buttercup Pl. RG18	39 E3
Cairngorm Rd. RG19	39 E5
Callard Dri. RG18	38 C3
Cedar Gro. RG19	38 D4
Celandine Gro. RG18	39 G4
Chapel Ct. RG18	39 F4
Chapel St. RG18	39 E4
Chapman Walk. RG18	38 C3
Charlock Clo. RG18	39 F2
Chesterton Rd. RG18	38 D2
Cholsey Rd. RG19	39 G4
Church Gate. RG19	39 E4
Church La. RG19	39 E4
Clerewater Pl. RG19	38 B4
Cochrane Clo. RG19	39 F4
Cold Ash Hill. RG18	38 D2
Coniston Clo. RG19	38 B4

Conway Dri. RG18 38 C2
Coombe Ct. RG19 39 F4
Coombe Clo. RG19 39 F4
Coombe Sq. RG19 39 F4
Coopers Cres. RG18 38 D3
Corderoy Clo. RG19 39 G5
Cowslip Cres. RG18 39 F2
*Crocus Mead,
 Harebell Dri. RG18 39 F3
Cropper Clo. RG19 39 H4
Crowfield Dri. RG18 38 C4
Crown Acre Clo. RG19 38 D4
Crown Mead. RG18 38 D4
Curlew Clo. RG19 38 D4
Cygnet Clo. RG19 38 C4
Danvers Clo. RG19 39 E5
Dart Clo. RG18 38 C2
Denton Clo. RG19 38 D5
Derwent Rd. RG19 38 C2
Dewberry Down. RG18 39 F3
Domoney Clo. RG19 39 F4
Doublet Clo. RG19 38 B4
Draper Clo. RG19 39 E5
Druce Way. RG19 39 E4
Dryden Clo. RG18 39 E2
Dunstan Rd. RG18 39 F3
Edwin Clo. RG19 39 G4
Eliot Clo. RG18 38 D2
Elm Av. RG19 39 F4
Elm Gro. RG18 38 C2
Elmhurst Rd. RG18 38 C2
Ennerdale Way. RG19 38 B4
Enterprise Way. RG19 39 H5
Ermine Walk. RG19 39 G5
Evreux Clo. RG19 39 G5
Exmoor Rd. RG19 38 D4
Falmouth Way. RG19 39 G4
Ferndale Ct. RG19 39 E4
Flag Staff Sq. RG19 39 F5
Flecker Clo. RG18 39 E2
Floral Way. RG18 39 G3
Fokerham Dri. RG19 39 G5
Foxglove Way. RG18 39 F3
Foxglove Way. RG18 39 F2
Foxhunter Way. RG19 38 B4
Fromont Dri. RG19 39 F4
Fuller Clo. RG19 39 G5
Fyfield Clo. RG19 39 G5
Fylingdales. RG19 38 D5
Glaisdale. RG19 38 D5
Glebelands. RG19 38 D4
Glenmore Clo. RG19 39 E6
Golding Clo. RG19 39 G4
Goldsmith Clo. RG18 38 D2
Goose Green Way.
 RG19 39 F4
Gordon Rd. RG18 38 B2
Grassington Pl. RG19 39 E5
Grassmead. RG19 39 G5
Great Barn Ct. RG19 39 G5
Green La. RG19 38 D4
Griffiths Clo. RG19 38 D5
Grindle Clo. RG18 38 D2
Halifax Pl. RG18 38 D3
Hambridge La. RG19 38 A5
Hammond Clo. RG19 39 G5
Hardy Ct. RG18 38 D2
Harebell Dri. RG18 39 F3
Hartley Way. RG18 39 F3
Hartmead Rd. RG19 39 F4
Harts Hill Rd. RG18 39 F3
Hatchgate Clo. RG18 38 D1
Hazel Gro. RG18 38 D4
Heardman Clo. RG19 39 G5
Heath La. RG18 39 E2
Heather Dri. RG19 39 E2
Hebden Clo. RG19 39 E6
Henwick Clo. RG18 38 C1
Henwick La. RG18 38 B2
Heron Way. RG19 38 C4
High St. RG19 39 E4
Holywell Ct. RG19 39 E4
Horne Rd. RG18 39 E5
Humber Clo. RG18 39 G4
Hurford Dri. RG19 39 G4
Ilkley Way. RG19 38 D5
INDUSTRIAL & RETAIL:
 Pipers Ind Est. RG19 39 G5
 The Berkshire Centre.
  RG19 39 H4
 Jedburgh Clo. RG19 39 F5
 John Hunt Clo. RG19 39 F5
*Jubilee Ct,
 Clerewater Pl. RG19 38 B4
Justice Clo. RG19 39 G5

Keighley Clo. RG19 38 D5
Kendal Clo. RG18 38 D3
Kennet Clo. RG19 39 F4
Kestrel Clo. RG19 38 C4
Kingsway. RG19 39 F5
Kipling Clo. RG18 38 D2
Lamb Clo. RG18 38 D2
Lancaster Clo. RG18 38 D3
Larkspur Gdns. RG18 39 G3
Lawrences La. RG18 39 E2
Lawrences Way. RG18 39 E2
Link Way. RG18 38 C3
Longbridge Rd. RG19 39 F5
Longcroft Rd. RG19 39 F5
Loundyes Clo. RG18 38 C3
Lower Farm Ct. RG19 38 B6
Lower Way. RG18 38 A4
Lyon Clo. RG19 39 G5
Magpie Clo. RG19 38 D4
Malham Rd. RG18 38 D4
Malthouse Clo. RG19 39 F5
Marsh Rd. RG18 39 F3
Masefield Rd. RG18 39 E3
Matthews Clo. RG19 38 D3
Maynard Clo. RG19 38 D4
Mayow Clo. RG19 39 G5
Meadow Clo. RG19 38 D4
Meadowsweet Clo.
 RG18 39 F3
Medway Clo. RG18 38 C2
Mersey Way. RG18 38 C2
Mill Reef Clo. RG19 38 B4
Montacute Dri. RG19 39 G5
Mount Rd. RG18 39 E3
Munkle Marsh. RG19 39 G4
Neville Dri. RG18 39 F4
Newbolt Clo. RG18 38 D2
Nideggen Clo. RG19 39 E4
Norlands. RG18 38 D2
Northfield Rd. RG18 38 D2
Northway. RG18 38 D2
Oak Tree Rd. RG19 39 F5
Park Av. RG18 39 E3
Park La. RG18 39 E2
Parkside Rd. RG18 39 E2
Pavy Clo. RG19 39 G5
Paynesdown Rd. RG19 38 C4
Peachey Clo. RG19 39 G5
Pegasus Clo. RG19 38 B3
Pentland Pl. RG19 38 D4
Pimpernel Pl. RG18 39 F3
Pipers La. RG18 39 G5
Pipers Way. RG18 39 G5
Pipit Clo. RG19 38 C4
Poffley Pl. RG19 38 C4
Poppy Dri. RG18 39 G3
Porlock Clo. RG19 39 E5
Pound La. RG18 38 B4
Prancing Horse Clo.
 RG18 39 F4
Prince Hold Rd. RG19 38 B4
Quarrington Clo. RG19 39 F5
Robertsfield. RG19 38 A4
Roman Way. RG18 38 C3
Rope Walk. RG18 39 D4
Rosedale Gdns. RG19 38 D5
Rosier Clo. RG18 39 G5
Rudland Clo. RG19 39 E5
Rydal Dri. RG18 38 B4
Sagecroft Rd. RG18 38 D3
St Johns Rd. RG18 38 D4
St Marks Clo. RG18 38 D4
Sargood Clo. RG19 39 F5
Saxon Ct. RG19 38 B4
Scrivens Mead. RG19 39 G4
Sedge Gro. RG18 39 F3
Severn Clo. RG18 38 C2
Shakespeare Rd. RG18 38 D3
Shelley Rd. RG18 38 D3
Simmons Field. RG18 39 G3
Skillman Dri. RG19 39 G4
Snowdon Clo. RG19 39 E5
Snowdrop Copse
 RG18 39 G3
Somerton Gro. RG18 38 D5
Southdown Rd. RG19 38 A4
Southend. RG18 38 D1
Spackman Clo. RG19 39 E5
Speedwell Way. RG18 39 G3
Spriggs Clo. RG18 39 E5
Spurcroft Rd. RG19 39 E5
Station Rd. RG18 39 E4
Stephenson Clo. RG18 39 E3
Stirling Way. RG18 38 D3

Stoney La. RG19 39 F4
Stroller Clo. RG19 38 B3
Sunderland Pl. RG18 38 D3
Swansdown Clo. RG19 38 C4
Swansdown Walk.
 RG18 38 C4
Sydney Clo. RG18 39 F4
Tadham Pl. RG19 38 D5
Tamarisk Ct. RG18 39 G3
Tarn Nowes Clo. RG19 38 B4
Tennyson Rd. RG18 38 D3
Thames Rd. RG18 38 C2
The Alders. RG18 39 E3
The Close. RG18 38 C3
The Firs. RG18 38 D3
The Frances. RG18 39 E3
The Grove. RG18 39 E3
The Haywards. RG18 39 E3
The Henrys. RG18 39 E3
The Hollands. RG18 39 F4
The Martins. RG19 39 G5
The Moors. RG19 39 E4
The Quantocks. RG19 39 E4
The Thackerays. RG19 39 E5
The Turnery. RG19 39 D4
The Waverleys. RG18 39 E4
Thompson Clo. RG18 39 F5
Tomlin Clo. RG19 39 F5
Trefoil Clo. RG19 39 F3
Trent Cres. RG18 38 C2
Tull Way. RG18 38 B3
Turners Rise. RG19 39 F4
Turnfields Rd. RG19 39 E4
Turnpike Rd. RG18 38 A3
Tyne Way. RG18 38 C2
Ullswater Clo. RG18 38 C4
Urquhart Rd. RG19 39 E6
Victor Rd. RG19 39 F4
Vincent Rd. RG18 39 F3
Violet Gro. RG18 39 F3
Walsingham Way. RG19 39 E5
Webbs Acre. RG19 39 G5
Wenlock Way. RG18 39 E5
Westerdale. RG19 39 E5
Westfield Cres. RG18 38 C3
Westfield Rd. RG18 38 C2
Westland. RG18 38 C3
Wheelers Grn Way.
 RG19 39 F5
Whitaker Clo. RG18 38 C3
Whitelands Rd. RG18 38 C3
Wilfred Way. RG19 39 G5
William Clo. RG19 38 E5
Windermere Way.
 RG19 38 C4
Winston Way. RG19 38 B4
Withybed Way. RG19 39 F2
Wordsworth Rd. RG18 38 D3

TWYFORD

Amberley Dri. RG10 40 A2
Arnside Clo. RG10 40 B2
Badger Clo. RG10 40 B1
Bell Ct. RG10 40 B4
Bolwell Clo. RG10 40 C5
Bridge Farm La. RG10 40 A2
Broad Hinton. RG10 40 A5
Broadwater Rd. RG10 40 C6
Brook St. RG10 40 B4
Burton Clo. RG10 40 C6
Byron Clo. RG10 40 B4
Byron Rd. RG10 40 B4
Carlile Gdns. RG10 40 B2
Castle End Rd. RG10 40 D3
Chapel Row. RG10 40 B4
Chaseside Av. RG10 40 B2
Cheriton Av. RG10 40 B2
Church La. RG10 40 D3
Church St. RG10 40 B4
Coleridge Clo. RG10 40 C6
Colleton Dri. RG10 40 C5
Cotterell Gdns. RG10 40 C5
Crest Clo. RG10 40 B2
Gas La. RG10 40 B4
Gooch Clo. RG10 40 C5
Harrison Clo. RG10 40 D5
Hermitage Dri. RG10 40 B2
Heron Dri. RG10 40 B2
High St. RG10 40 A4
Highgrove Pl. RG10 40 C3
Hilltop Rd. RG10 40 B2

Hogmoor La. RG10 40 C6
Hubbard Clo. RG10 40 C6
Hurst Park Rd. RG10 40 C6
Hurst Rd. RG10 40 B4
INDUSTRIAL & RETAIL:
 Ruscombe Park Ind Est.
  RG10 40 C3
Jarvis Dri. RG10 40 B2
Kibblewhite Cres. RG10 40 B2
Kingfisher Ct. RG10 40 C5
Lincoln Gdns. RG10 40 B3
Llewelllyn Pk. RG10 40 A2
Loddon Hall Rd. RG10 40 B3
Loddon Vw. RG10 40 B5
London Rd. RG10 40 B4
Longfield Rd. RG10 40 B3
Mallard Clo. RG10 40 C5
Malvern Way. RG10 40 B2
Maple Bank. RG10 40 C3
Middlefields. RG10 40 C2
Milton Way. RG10 40 D3
New Bath Rd. RG10 40 B4
New Rd. RG10 40 B2
New Rd,
 Ruscombe. RG10 40 C2
Northbury Av. RG10 40 C3
Northbury La. RG10 40 C3
Old Bath Rd,
 Charvil. RG10 40 A4
Old Bath Rd,
 Ruscombe. RG10 40 C3
Old Mill Clo. RG10 40 B4
Orchard Est. RG10 40 C3
Packham Dri. RG10 40 B2
Paddock Heights. RG10 40 B5
Pennfields. RG10 40 B2
Pine Gro. RG10 40 B3
Polehampton Clo. RG10 40 B4
Polehampton Ct. RG10 40 B4
Poundfield Way. RG10 40 D6
Royal Station Ct. RG10 40 B4
Ruscombe La. RG10 40 C3
Ruscombe Pk. RG10 40 C3
Ruscombe Rd. RG10 40 B3
St James Clo. RG10 40 C3
St Michaels Ct. RG10 40 B2
St Swithins Ct. RG10 40 B2
Saunders Clo. RG10 40 C6
Silk La. RG10 40 A4
South View Clo. RG10 40 B2
Southbury La. RG10 40 D3
Springfield Pk. RG10 40 C4
Stanlake La. RG10 40 C4
Station Rd. RG10 40 B4
Stephen Clo. RG10 40 C6
Swans Ct. RG. RG10 40 C5
Sycamore Rd. RG10 40 B3
The Grove. RG10 40 B4
The Pines. RG10 40 B1
Thornbury Grn. RG10 40 B3
Treacher Ct. RG10 40 C3
Troutbeck Clo. RG10 40 B2
Verey Clo. RG10 40 C5
Wagtail Clo. RG10 40 B4
Walnut Tree Clo. RG10 40 C2
Waltham Rd,
 Ruscombe. RG10 40 C3
Waltham Rd,
 Twyford. RG10 40 B4
Wargrave Rd. RG10 40 A1
Waterside Ct. RG10 40 A4
Weavers Way. RG10 40 A4
Wensley Clo. RG10 40 B3
Wessex Gdns. RG10 40 C5
Westview Rd. RG10 40 B2
Willow Clo. RG10 40 B2
Winchcombe Rd. RG10 40 B5
Woodpecker Clo. RG10 40 C5
Yewhurst Clo. RG10 40 A2

UXBRIDGE

Alder Rd. UB9 41 A1
Alexandra Rd. UB8 41 B6
Austin Waye. UB8 41 A5
Bakers Rd. UB8 41 B3
Bakers Yd. UB8 41 B3
Barnfield Pl. UB8 41 A4
Bassett Rd. UB8 41 A3
Bawtree Rd. UB8 41 B3
Beasleys Yd. UB8 41 B3
Belmont Clo. UB8 41 C2

Belmont Rd. UB8 41 B3
Bettles Clo. UB8 41 A5
*Black Horse Pl,
 Waterloo Rd 41 A4
Blackmore Way. UB8 41 B2
Braybourne Clo. UB8 41 A2
Brearley Clo. UB8 41 D1
Bridge Rd. UB8 41 A6
Burness Clo. UB8 41 C6
Cambridge Rd. UB8 41 B1
Caxton Dri. UB8 41 B6
Chapel St. UB8 41 B4
Charter Pl. UB8 41 B4
Chequers Sq. UB8 41 B3
Chiltern View Rd. UB8 41 B6
Chippendale All. UB8 41 C4
Chippendale Waye.
 UB8 41 C3
Cobden Clo. UB8 41 A4
Concorde Clo. UB10 41 D6
Cornfield Clo. UB8 41 C6
Cornwall Rd. UB8 41 C1
Cotswold Clo. UB8 41 B5
Cowley Mill Rd. UB8 41 A6
Cowley Rd. UB8 41 B6
Cricketfield Rd. UB8 41 B4
Cross St. UB8 41 B4
Crown Walk. UB8 41 B3
Cumbrian Way. UB8 41 C4
Dawes Rd. UB10 41 D6
Derby Rd. UB8 41 B5
*Dukes Way,
 Waterloo Rd. UB8 41 A4
Elm Lawn Clo. UB8 41 D2
Fairfield Rd. UB8 41 B1
Fairlight Dri. UB8 41 B1
Fassnidge Vw. UB8 41 A3
Frays Waye. UB8 41 A4
Gatting Way. UB8 41 D1
George St. UB8 41 C3
Glebe Rd. UB8 41 A6
Grainges Yd. UB8 41 B3
Grays Rd. UB10 41 D4
Grove Rd. UB8 41 C3
Grove Waye. UB8 41 C3
Harefield Rd. UB8 41 B2
Hawthorn Rd. UB9 41 A1
Heron Clo. UB8 41 C1
High St. UB8 41 B3
Hillingdon Rd. UB10 41 B4
Hinton Rd. UB8 41 B4
Honeycroft Hill. UB10 41 D3
Hows Clo. UB8 41 A4
Hows Rd. UB8 41 A4
Iffley Rd. UB8 41 C3
INDUSTRIAL & RETAIL:
 The Chimes Shopping
  Centre. UB8 41 B3
Jackson Clo. UB10 41 D3
Jackson Rd. UB10 41 D3
Kent Clo. UB8 41 B1
Lancaster Rd. UB8 41 B2
Lancresse Clo. UB8 41 B2
Lawn Rd. UB8 41 A4
Manor Waye. UB8 41 C5
Market Sq. UB8 41 B3
Martin Clo. UB10 41 D6
Maylands Dri. UB8 41 C1
Mead Rd. UB8 41 C2
Medman Clo. UB8 41 B6
Mercer Walk. UB8 41 B3
Merry Fields. UB8 41 C6
Mill Av. UB8 41 A6
Mill Bridge Pl. UB8 41 A6
*Millennium Clo,
 Waterloo Rd. UB8 41 A4
Montague Rd. UB8 41 C3
Myddleton Rd. UB8 41 B5
Nashs Yd. UB8 41 B3
New Winsdor St. UB8 41 A4
Norfolk Rd. UB8 41 C2
Nursery Waye. UB8 41 C5
Nutkin Wk. UB10 41 D3
Orchard Waye. UB8 41 C6
Osborn Rd. UB8 41 A1
Oxford Rd. UB8 41 A1
Pages La. UB8 41 B1
Pantile Walk. UB8 41 C4
Park Rd. UB8 41 C6
Park Rd E. UB8 41 C6
Penrith Clo. UB8 41 C1
Press Rd. UB8 41 C1
Redfern Clo. UB8 41 A4
Redford Way. UB8 41 B3

Rockingham Clo. UB8 41 A4
Rockingham Rd. UB8 41 A4
Rushes Mead. UB8 41 A4
St Andrews Rd. UB10 41 D4
St Lukes Rd. UB10 41 D4
Sanderson Rd. UB8 41 A2
Sidney Clo. UB8 41 A4
South Common Rd. UB8 41 D1
Stanley Clo. UB8 41 B5
Tachbrook Rd. UB8 41 A6
The Greenway. UB8 41 B6
The Hermitage. UB8 41 C2
The Lynch. UB8 41 A3
Thompson Rd. UB10 41 D4
Trumper Way. UB8 41 A4
Turnpike. UB10 41 D6
Valley Rd. UB10 41 D6
Victoria Rd. UB8 41 A3
Vine St. UB8 41 B4
Walford Rd. UB8 41 B6
Wallace Clo. UB10 41 D6
Warwick Pl. UB8 41 B2
Waterloo Rd. UB8 41 A4
Wellington Clo. UB8 41 A4
West Common Rd. UB8 41 C1
Westcott Waye. UB8 41 A5
Whitehall Clo. UB8 41 B4
Whitehall Rd. UB8 41 B4
Willow Av. UB9 41 A1
Wilmar Rd. UB8 41 B2
Windsor St. UB8 41 B4
Wyvern Way. UB8 41 A4
York Rd. UB8 41 C3

WARGRAVE

utumn Walk. RG10 42 B5
Backsideans. RG10 42 B5
Bayliss Rd. RG10 42 B6
Beverley Gdns. RG10 42 C6
Blakes Rd. RG10 42 C5
Braybrooke Gdns. RG10 42 B6
Braybrooke Rd. RG10 42 B6
hurch St. RG10 42 B5
lifton Rise. RG10 42 C5
Dark La. RG10 42 C5
Dunnock Way. RG10 42 C4
ast View Clo. RG10 42 D5
ast View Rd. RG10 42 D5
lizabeth Ct. RG10 42 C5
mma La. RG10 42 C5
erry La. RG10 42 B5
idlers Walk. RG10 42 C5
Hamilton Rd. RG10 42 C5
High St. RG10 42 B6
Highfield Pk. RG10 42 D4
Hill Lands. RG10 42 B5
anghams Way. RG10 42 C5
oddon Dri. RG10 42 A6
McCraes Wk. RG10 42 C5
Mumbery Hill. RG10 42 C6
Newalls Rise. RG10 42 C5
urfield Dri. RG10 42 C5
ecreation Rd. RG10 42 C5
idge Way. RG10 42 C5
yecroft Clo. RG10 42 C5
chool Hill. RG10 42 C5
chool La. RG10 42 B5
ilverdale Rd. RG10 42 C6
pring Walk. RG10 42 B5
tation Rd. RG10 42 A5
he Bothy. RG10 42 B5
he Copse. RG10 42 C4
he Spur. RG10 42 C4
he Vinery. RG10 42 B5
he Walled Gdn. RG10 42 B5
wyford Rd. RG10 42 B6
ictoria Rd. RG10 42 C5
Vargrave Hill. RG10 42 B5
Vatermans Wy. RG10 42 A6
Villow La. RG10 42 B4

WICK HILL/ FINCHAMPSTEAD

rnett Clo. RG40 43 B3
very Clo. RG40 43 C4
ankside. RG40 43 C4
arkham Ride. RG40 43 A2
Billing Av. RG40 43 B4
Birch Rd. RG40 43 C3
Booth Dri. RG40 43 B2
Briarwood. RG40 43 A4
Buchanan Dri. RG40 43 B3
Burchett Coppice. RG40 43 B2
Burnt Oak. RG40 43 C2
Cambrian Way. RG40 43 D2
Carolina Pl. RG40 43 A3
Cart Clo. RG40 43 B4
Challenor Clo. RG40 43 B3
Charlton Clo. RG40 43 B2
Chivers Dri. RG40 43 B3
Church Hams. RG40 43 A4
Church La. RG40 43 B6
Columbia Ct. RG40 43 A3
Copse Way. RG40 43 A3
Croft Rd. RG40 43 C1
Cypress Clo. RG40 43 D2
Ditchfield La. RG40 43 B2
Dodsells Well. RG40 43 B2
Drake Clo. RG40 43 B3
Elgarth Dri. RG40 43 B2
Fernbank. RG40 43 A4
Finchampstead Rd. RG40 43 B5
Fir Cottage Rd. RG40 43 B2
Firs Clo. RG40 43 B4
Foxcote. RG40 43 C4
Garret Rd. RG40 43 B2
Garston Gro. RG40 43 B2
Gibbs Clo. RG40 43 B4
Gilbert Wy. RG40 43 A2
Goldsmiths Clo. RG40 43 B1
Gorse Ride Nth. RG40 43 B3
Gorse Ride Sth. RG40 43 B4
Hazelbank. RG40 43 A4
Heath Ride. RG40 43 C4
Heather Clo. RG40 43 A3
Ingle Glen. RG40 43 C3
Jerrymoor Hill. RG40 43 C3
Johnson Dri. RG40 43 D3
Jubilee Rd. RG40 43 B6
Kelsey Av. RG40 43 B4
Kiln Ride. RG40 43 C2
McCarthey Way. RG40 43 B2
Manor Park Dri. RG40 43 A4
Maryland Clo. RG40 43 A3
Masdar Gdns. RG40 43 A4
Merryweather Clo. RG40 43 B2
Moor Clo. RG40 43 A3
Mornington Av. RG40 43 B2
Nashgrove La. RG40 43 B1
Ninemile Ride. RG40 43 A4
Orbit Clo. RG40 43 B4
Oregon Walk. RG40 43 A3
Pine Dri. RG40 43 C3
Radical Ride. RG40 43 B3
Range Rd. RG40 43 D3
Redgauntlet. RG40 43 A4
Roycroft La. RG40 43 B2
Royston Gdns. RG40 43 C4
Russley Grn. RG40 43 C1
St James Rd. RG40 43 A2
Sandhurst Rd. RG40 43 D2
Shenstone Clo. RG40 43 C2
Springdale. RG40 43 B2
Summit Clo. RG40 43 C4
Tanglewood. RG40 43 C3
The Dittons. RG40 43 B4
The Lea. RG40 43 B2
The Lodges. RG40 43 B3
The Spinney. RG40 43 B2
Thomas La. RG40 43 B2
Ticknor Dri. RG40 43 C3
Tintagel Rd. RG40 43 D2
Tomlinson Dri. RG40 43 D4
Vermont Woods. RG40 43 A3
Vicarage Clo. RG40 43 B4
Warren Clo. RG40 43 B4
Warren La. RG40 43 A5
Washington Gdns. RG40 43 C3
Watkins Clo. RG40 43 B3
Watson Clo. RG40 43 B1
Waverley Way. RG40 43 B1
White Horse La. RG40 43 A5
Whittle Clo. RG40 43 B4
Wick Hill La. RG40 43 C4
Wild Briar. RG40 43 C3
Wildcroft Dri. RG40 43 C1
Willow Dale. RG40 43 B3
Wimbushes. RG40 43 A4
Windsor Ride. RG40 43 C3
Woodside Clo. RG40 43 A2

WINDSOR & ETON

Abbotts Walk. SL4 46 C4
Addington Clo. SL4 47 E5
Adelaide Sq. SL4 47 H4
Albany Rd. SL4 47 G4
Albert Rd. SL4 47 H5
Albert St. SL4 47 F3
Alden Vw. SL4 46 B3
Alexandra Ct. SL4 47 G4
Alexandra Rd. SL4 47 G4
Alider Mans. SL4 46 B3
Allkins Ct. SL4 47 H4
Alma Rd. SL4 47 G4
Almond Clo. SL4 47 F4
Arthur Rd. SL4 47 F3
Ash La. SL4 46 B4
Aston Mead. SL4 46 C3
Atherton Ct. SL4 47 G2
Athlone Sq. SL4 47 G3
Bachelors Acre. SL4 47 H3
Bailey Clo. SL4 47 E4
Baldwins Shore. SL4 47 G1
Ballard Grn. SL4 46 C2
Balmoral Gdns. SL4 47 G5
Barry Av. SL4 47 G2
Basford Way. SL4 46 B5
Beaumont Rd. SL4 47 G4
Bell Par. SL. SL4 46 D4
Bell Vw. SL4 46 D5
Bell View Clo. SL4 46 D4
Benning Clo. SL4 46 B5
Bexley St. SL4 47 F3
Birch Gro. SL4 46 B3
Birchington Rd. SL4 47 E4
Black Horse Clo. SL4 46 B4
Bolton Av. SL4 47 G5
Bolton Cres. SL4 47 G5
Bolton Rd. SL4 47 G5
Bourne Av. SL4 47 G5
Bowes-Lyon Clo. SL4 47 G3
Bradshaw Clo. SL4 46 C3
Bridgeman Dri. SL4 47 E4
Bridgewater Ter. SL4 47 G3
Brocas St. SL4 47 G2
Brook St. SL4 47 H4
Brudenell. SL4 46 D5
Bryer Pl. SL4 46 B5
Buckland Cres. SL4 46 D3
Bulkeley Av. SL4 47 F4
Burnetts Rd. SL4 46 C3
Burnham Clo. SL4 46 B4
Burton Way. SL4 46 C5
Butlers Clo. SL4 46 B3
Byron Ct. SL4 47 E5
Carey Clo. SL4 47 F5
Carter Clo. SL4 47 E4
Castle Hill. SL4 47 H3
Cavalry Cres. SL4 47 F5
Cawcott Dri. SL4 46 C3
Chantry Clo. SL4 47 E3
Charles St. SL4 47 G3
Charlton. SL4 46 A4
Chaucer Clo. SL4 47 H5
Chestnut Dri. SL4 46 D6
Christian Sq. SL4 47 G3
Church Clo. SL4 47 G1
Church La. SL4 47 H3
Church St. SL4 47 H3
Church Ter. SL4 46 C4
Claremont Rd. SL4 47 G4
Clarence Cres. SL4 47 G3
Clarence Rd. SL4 47 F3
Cleve Ct. SL4 46 D5
Clewer Av. SL4 47 E4
Clewer Ct. SL4 47 E2
Clewer New Town. SL4 47 E4
Clewer Pk. SL4 47 E2
Clewer Rd, Clewer. SL4 47 E2
Clewer Rd, Windsor. SL4 46 C4
Clifton Rise. SL4 46 B3
College Cres. SL4 47 F4
Convent Rd. SL4 46 D4
Coombe Hill Ct. SL4 46 C6
Coombemere Clo. SL4 47 F4
Copper Beech Clo. SL4 46 B3
Cranbourne Av. SL4 46 D4
Cross Oak. SL4 47 E4
Dagmar Rd. SL4 47 G4
Datchet St. SL4 47 H2
Dawson Clo. SL4 47 E4
Dean Clo. SL4 46 B5
Dedworth Dri. SL4 46 D3
Dedworth Rd. SL4 46 A4
Devereux Rd. SL4 47 G4
Dorset Rd. SL4 47 G4
Dower Pk. SL4 46 C6
Duke St. SL4 47 F2
Duncannon Cres. SL4 46 B5
Duncroft. SL4 46 D5
Dyson Clo. SL4 47 F5
East Cres. SL4 46 D3
Edinburgh Gdns. SL4 47 H5
Ellison Dri. SL4 46 D5
Elm Rd. SL4 47 F5
Errington Dri. SL4 47 E3
Eton Ct. SL4 47 G2
Eton Sq. SL4 47 H2
Etonwick Rd. SL4 47 H1
Fairacres. SL4 46 B4
Fairlawn Pk. SL4 46 C6
Fairlight Av. SL4 47 H4
Farm Yd. SL4 47 H2
Fawcett Rd. SL4 47 F3
Filmer Rd. SL4 46 B4
Firs Av. SL4 46 D5
Forest Rd. SL4 46 C4
Foster Av. SL4 46 C5
Fountain Gdns. SL4 47 H5
Frances Rd. SL4 47 G5
Frances St. SL4 47 G4
Franklyn Cres. SL4 46 B5
Frymley Way. SL4 46 B3
Furness. SL4 46 A4
Gallys Rd. SL4 46 B3
Gilman Cres. SL4 46 B5
Gloucester Pl. SL4 47 H4
Gordon Rd. SL4 46 D5
Goslar Way. SL4 47 F4
Goswell Hill. SL4 47 G3
Goswell Rd. SL4 47 G3
Gratton Dri. SL4 46 C6
Green Acre. SL4 46 C4
Green La. SL4 47 E4
Grove Rd. SL4 47 G4
Guards Rd. SL4 46 B4
Gwynne Clo. SL4 46 C3
Hanley Clo. SL4 46 B3
Hanover Way. SL4 46 D3
Harcourt Rd. SL4 46 C3
Harrington Clo. SL4 46 D6
Haslemere Rd. SL4 47 E3
Hatch La. SL4 46 D5
Hatton Ct. SL4 47 F4
Hawtrey Rd. SL4 47 G4
Hayse Hill. SL4 46 B3
Helena Rd. SL4 47 H4
Helston La. SL4 47 E3
Hemwood Rd. SL4 46 B5
Hermitage La. SL4 47 E5
High St, Eton. SL4 47 G1
High St, Windsor. SL4 47 H3
Highfield. SL4 46 D5
Holly Cres. SL4 46 B4
Homers Rd. SL4 46 B3
Hylle Clo. SL4 46 C3
Illingworth. SL4 46 C5
Imperial Rd. SL4 47 E5
INDUSTRIAL & RETAIL:
Fairacres Ind Est. SL4 46 C6
Vansittart Ind Area. SL4 47 F3
*Jubilee Arch, Peascod St. SL4 47 H3
Jacobs Clo. SL4 46 C3
James St. SL4 47 G3
Keats La. SL4 47 G1
Keeler Clo. SL4 46 C5
Keepers Farm Clo. SL4 46 C4
Kenneally. SL4 46 A4
Kentons La. SL4 46 C4
Keppel St. SL4 47 H4
Kimber Clo. SL4 46 D5
King Edwart Ct. SL4 47 G3
King Edward VII Av. SL4 47 H2
Kings Field. SL4 46 B3
Kings Rd. SL4 47 H4
Kingstable St. SL4 47 H2
Knights Clo. SL4 46 B3
Lammas Ct. SL4 47 G4
Leigh Sq. SL4 46 B4
Liddell Pl. SL4 46 B5
Little Buntings. SL4 46 D5
Lodge Way. SL4 46 C5
Longmead. SL4 46 C3
Loring Rd. SL4 46 D3
Losfield Rd. SL4 46 C3
Lovejoy La. SL4 46 B4
Luff Clo. SL4 46 C5
Lyell. SL4 46 A5
Madeira Walk. SL4 47 H3
Maidenhead Rd. SL4 46 A3
Manor Farm Clo. SL4 46 D5
Manor Rd. SL4 46 C4
Mansell Clo. SL4 46 C3
Marbeck Clo. SL4 46 B3
Martins Clo. SL4 46 B3
Meadow La. SL4 47 F1
Mellor Wk. SL4 47 G3
Merwin Way. SL4 46 B4
Mill La. SL4 47 E2
Monks Rd. SL4 46 B4
Montpelier. SL4 47 G4
Mountbatten Sq. SL4 47 G3
Needham Clo. SL4 46 C3
Nelson Rd. SL4 46 D5
Newberry Cres. SL4 46 B4
Nicholls. SL4 46 A5
Nightingale Wk. SL4 47 G5
North Clo. SL4 46 D3
Oak La. SL4 47 E3
Oakley Grn Rd. SL4 46 A3
Orchard Av. SL4 47 E3
Orwell Clo. SL4 47 G5
Osborne Ct. SL4 47 G4
Osborne Mews. SL4 47 G4
Osborne Rd. SL4 47 G4
Oxford Rd. SL4 47 F3
Oxford St. SL4 47 G3
Park Clo. SL4 47 H4
Park Corner. SL4 46 C5
Park St. SL4 47 H3
Parsonage La. SL4 47 E3
Peascod St. SL4 47 G3
Peel Clo. SL4 47 E5
Perrycroft. SL4 46 C5
Pierson Rd. SL4 46 B3
Poolmans Rd. SL4 46 B5
Prince Consort Cotts. SL4 47 G4
Princess Av. SL4 47 F5
Priors Rd. SL4 46 B5
Queen Annes Rd. SL4 47 G6
Queens Acre. SL4 47 G6
Queens Rd. SL4 47 G4
Rays Av. SL4 46 D2
Rectory Clo. SL4 47 E3
Redford Rd. SL4 46 B3
Regent Ct. SL4 47 H4
River St. SL4 47 G2
Riverside Walk. SL4 47 H2
Romney Lock Rd. SL4 47 H2
Roses La. SL4 46 C4
Rowland Clo. SL4 46 B5
Ruddlesway. SL4 46 B3
Russel St. SL4 47 G3
Rutherford Clo. SL4 46 D4
Rydings. SL4 46 C5
Ryecroft. SL4 46 D5
St Albans St. SL4 47 H3
St Andrews Av. SL4 46 D4
St Andrews Cres. SL4 46 D4
St Georges Clo. SL4 46 C3
St Johns Dri. SL4 46 D4
St Johns Rd. SL4 47 E4
St Leonards Av. SL4 47 G4
St Leonards Hill. SL4 46 C5
St Leonards Rd. SL4 47 G4
St Marks Pl. SL4 47 G4
St Marks Rd. SL4 47 G4
Sawyers Clo. SL4 46 C2
Sheepcote Rd. SL4 46 C4
Sheet St. SL4 47 H4
Sherbourne Dri. SL4 46 D6
Shirley Av. SL4 46 D3
Shirley Hall Clo. SL4 46 D3
Sidney Rd. SL4 46 A5
Sinclair Rd. SL4 47 G5
Smiths La. SL4 46 C4
Snowdon Clo. SL4 46 B6
South Meadow La. SL4 47 G2
Spinners Walk. SL4 47 G3
Springfield Clo. SL4 47 F4
Springfield Rd. SL4 47 F4

Stephenson Dri. SL4 47 E2
Stirling Clo. SL4 46 B4
Stovell Rd. SL4 47 F2
Stroud Clo. SL4 46 B5
Stuart Clo. SL4 46 B4
Stuart Way. SL4 46 C4
Sun Clo. SL4 47 G1
Sunbury Rd. SL4 47 H1
Sycamore Ct. SL4 47 G5
Tangier Ct. SL4 47 H1
Tangier La. SL4 47 H1
Tarbay La. SL4 46 A4
Temple Rd. SL4 47 G4
Testwood Rd. SL4 46 B3
Thames Av. SL4 47 H2
Thames Mead. SL4 46 C3
Thames Side. SL4 47 H2
Thames St. SL4 47 H2
The Hatch. SL4 46 A2
The Limes. SL4 46 A4
The Parade. SL4 46 B3
Tinkers La. SL4 46 B4
Trinity Pl. SL4 47 G4
Tudor Way. SL4 46 C3
Turnoak Park. SL4 46 C5
Tyrell Gdns. SL4 46 D5
Upcroft. SL4 47 E5
Vale Rd. SL4 46 D2
Vansittart Rd. SL4 47 F3
Victor Rd. SL4 47 G5
Victoria St. SL4 47 G3
Washington Dri. SL4 46 C5
Wells Ct. SL4 47 E3
West Cres. SL4 46 D3
Westmead. SL4 47 F5
White Horse Rd. SL4 46 B5
White Lilies Island. SL4 47 E2
Whiteley Clo. SL4 46 C2
William St. SL4 47 G3
Willow Gro. SL4 47 E5
Wilton Cres. SL4 46 B5
Windmill Clo. SL4 47 F4
Winkfield Rd. SL4 46 D6
Witney Clo. SL4 46 C3
Wolf La. SL4 46 B5
Wood Clo. SL4 47 G6
Woodland Av. SL4 46 D6
Wright. SL4 46 B5
Wyatt Clo. SL4 46 B5
York Av. SL4 47 F4
York Rd. SL4 47 F4

WINNERSH

Acorn Gdns. RG41 44 A2
Albany Park Dri. RG41 44 A2
Alderney Gdns. RG41 44 C2
Allnatt Av. RG41 44 B3
Annesley Gdns. RG41 44 B2
Arbor La. RG41 44 A2
Arbor Mdws. RG41 44 A2
Arun Clo. RG41 44 A2
Ashton Rd. RG41 44 E3
Astor Clo. RG41 44 C2
Azalea Clo. RG41 44 A3
Baslow Rd. RG41 44 A2
Bathurst Rd. RG41 44 A2
Bayley Ct. RG41 44 B4
Bearwood Path. RG41 44 A2
Bearwood Rd. RG41 44 A4
Beckford Clo. RG41 44 E3
Birchmead. RG41 44 C2
Bluebell Meadow.
 RG41 44 B1
Borrowdale Rd. RG41 44 A1
Bredon Rd. RG41 44 E4
Brimblecombe Clo.
 RG41 44 F4
Cantley Cres. RG41 44 F4
Chackfield Dri. RG41 44 C4
Chatsworth Av. RG41 44 A2
Church Clo. RG41 44 B2
Churchill Dri. RG41 44 A3
Clarendon Clo. RG41 44 C3
Clifton Rd. RG41 44 F4
Commons Rd. RG41 44 E4
Cornfield Grn. RG41 44 E4
Danywern Dri. RG41 44 B3
Davis Clo. RG41 44 A3
Davis St. RG10 44 C1
Davis Way. RG10 44 C1
Deerhurst Av. RG41 44 B2

Defford Clo. RG41 44 E4
Delane Dri. RG41 44 A3
Dolphin Clo. RG41 44 B4
Donnation Pl. RG41 44 C3
Douglas Grange. RG10 44 C1
Dunstans Way. RG41 44 A3
Dunt Av. RG10 44 D1
Dunt La. RG10 44 D1
Eastbury Pk. RG41 44 C3
Eden Way. RG41 44 A3
Elmley Clo. RG41 44 E4
Emm Clo. RG41 44 E4
Emmbrook Gate. RG41 44 E4
Emmbrook Rd. RG41 44 E4
Emmbrook Vale. RG41 44 F3
Eskdale Rd. RG41 44 A1
Field Way. RG41 44 C2
Fulbrook Clo. RG41 44 F4
Garth Clo. RG41 44 B3
Goddard Ct. RG41 44 B4
Grasmere Clo. RG41 44 B4
Green La,
 Hurst. RG10 44 D1
Green La,
 Winnersh. RG41 44 C2
Greenwood Gro. RG41 44 C2
Grovelands Av. RG41 44 C2
Grovelands Rd. RG41 44 C2
Harefield Clo. RG41 44 C2
Harman Ct. RG41 44 A3
INDUSTRIAL & RETAIL:
 Winnersh Triangle
 Ind Est. RG41 44 A1
Isis Clo. RG41 44 A3
Kelburne Clo. RG41 44 B2
King Street La. RG41 44 A4
Laburnum Rd. RG41 44 B4
Lenham Clo. RG41 44 B4
Little Hill Rd. RG10 44 C1
Longdon Rd. RG41 44 B4
Lowther Clo. RG41 44 E4
Lowther Rd. RG41 44 E4
Maidensfield. RG41 44 C3
Maple Clo. RG41 44 C1
Marks Rd. RG41 44 F4
Matthews Green Rd.
 RG41 44 F4
Mayfields. RG41 44 A4
Meadow Vw. RG41 44 C1
Melbourne Av. RG41 44 B3
Melody Clo. RG41 44 B2
Mermaid Clo. RG41 44 C1
Merryhill Chase. RG41 44 C1
Merryhill Green La.
 RG41 44 C1
New Rd. RG41 44 A4
Old Forest Rd. RG41 44 D4
Overbury Av. RG41 44 E4
Pheasant Clo. RG41 44 B3
Poplar La. RG41 44 C2
Primrose La. RG41 44 B1
Priory Ct. RG41 44 C2
Rainbow Pk. RG41 44 B3
Reading Rd. RG41 44 A2
Reynards Clo. RG41 44 C3
Robin Hood La. RG41 44 B3
Robin Hood Way. RG41 44 C2
Roundabout La. RG41 44 D4
Russell Way. RG41 44 A3
Sadlers Ct. RG41 44 C4
Sadlers La. RG41 44 C4
St Catherines Clo. RG41 44 A4
St Marys Rd. RG41 44 A4
Sandstone Clo. RG41 44 B4
Sewell Av. RG41 44 F4
Sherwood Rd. RG41 44 C2
Simons La. RG41 44 D4
Sindle Clo. RG41 44 A3
Snowdrop Gro. RG41 44 B2
Summerfield Clo. RG41 44 F3
Sylvester Clo. RG41 44 B4
Targett Ct. RG41 44 A3
The Metro Centre. RG41 44 F3
The Priory. RG41 44 C2
Toutley Clo. RG41 44 E4
Toutley Rd. RG41 44 F3
Turnstone Clo. RG41 44 A2
Watmore La. RG41 44 C4
Wedderburn Clo. RG41 44 C3
Welby Cres. RG41 44 B3
Westfield Rd. RG41 44 A3
Wharfedale Rd. RG41 44 A1
Wilson Clo. RG41 44 B3
Windermere Clo. RG41 44 B2

Winnersh Gate. RG41 44 C3
Winnersh Gro. RG41 44 B3
Woodhurst La. RG41 44 F4
Woodlands Av. RG41 44 D4
Woodward Clo. RG41 44 C3

WOKINGHAM

Abbey Clo. RG40 49 E2
Acorn Dri. RG40 49 E2
Agate Clo. RG41 48 A2
Agincourt Clo. RG40 48 B3
Albert Rd. RG40 48 D4
Alderman Willey Clo.
 RG41 48 D3
All Saints Clo. RG40 49 E1
Amethyst Clo. RG41 48 A2
Andrew Clo. RG40 49 G4
Antares Clo. RG41 48 B3
Apple Clo. RG41 48 B4
Aquila Clo. RG41 48 B3
Arnold Clo. RG40 49 H2
Arthur Rd. RG41 48 C3
Ashridge Rd. RG40 49 F1
Ashville Way. RG41 48 D4
Astley Clo. RG41 48 B2
Banbury Clo. RG41 48 D3
Barkham Rd. RG41 48 A6
Barkhart Dri. RG40 49 E2
Barrett Cres. RG40 49 F3
Battys Barn Clo. RG40 49 F4
Beale Clo. RG40 49 E2
Bean Oak Rd. RG40 49 G3
Beaver Clo. RG41 48 D5
Beckett Clo. RG40 49 G3
Bedford Gdns. RG41 48 B3
Bedfordshire Way.
 RG41 48 A3
Beechnut Clo. RG41 48 B4
Bell Foundry La. RG40 49 E1
Benning Rd. RG40 49 F1
Beryl Clo. RG41 48 A2
Binfield Rd. RG40 49 G3
Bird Mews. RG40 49 E3
Bishops Dri. RG40 49 E2
Blagrove Dri. RG41 48 C5
Blagrove La. RG41 48 C5
Blake Clo. RG40 49 G1
Blandford Dri. RG41 48 B5
Blenheim Clo. RG41 48 B3
Bowyer Cres. RG40 49 F1
Bridge Clo. RG41 48 B2
Broad St. RG40 49 E3
Broad St Wk. RG40 49 E3
Brook Clo. RG41 48 C1
Brookside. RG41 48 C2
Broom Gro. RG41 48 A5
Buckhurst Gro. RG40 49 H4
Buckthorn Clo. RG41 48 A2
Budges Gdns. RG40 49 G2
Budges Rd. RG40 49 F1
Bush Walk. RG40 49 E3
Buttercup Clo. RG40 49 H2
Cambridgeshire Clo.
 RG41 48 A3
Camelia Way. RG41 48 A2
Campion Way. RG40 49 G2
Cantley Cres. RG40 49 C1
Carey Rd. RG40 49 E4
Caroline Dri. RG41 48 C2
Cedar Clo. RG40 49 E2
Central Walk. RG40 49 E3
Chackfield Dri. RG41 48 A1
Chaffinch Clo. RG40 49 F1
Charwood Rd. RG40 49 G3
Chaucer Clo. RG40 49 H2
Chaucer Way. RG41 48 A4
Cheeseman Clo. RG40 49 F2
Chestnut Av. RG41 48 A3
Chetwode Clo. RG40 49 G3
Child Clo. RG40 49 E2
Clare Av. RG40 49 E2
Clay La. RG40 49 H3
Clifton Rd. RG41 48 C1
Clover Clo. RG40 49 G2
Cockpit Path. RG40 49 E4
Comfrey Clo. RG40 49 H2
Copse Dri. RG41 48 C2
Cornflower Clo. RG41 48 A2
Cornwall Clo. RG41 48 A3
Coronation Sq. RG40 49 F2

Crail Clo. RG41 48 D6
Crecy Clo. RG41 48 A3
Crescent Rd. RG40 49 E4
Crocus Clo. RG41 48 A2
Cross St. RG40 49 F3
Crutchley Rd. RG40 49 F2
Culloden Way. RG41 48 A3
Cumberland Way. RG41 48 A3
Curl Way. RG41 48 C4
Davy Clo. RG40 49 E4
De Vitre Grn. RG40 49 H2
Deacon Clo. RG40 49 E1
Dean Gro. RG40 49 E2
Denmark St. RG40 49 E4
Denton Rd. RG40 49 E3
Derwent Clo. RG41 48 B3
Devon Clo. RG41 48 A3
Diamond Way. RG41 48 A2
Dieppe Clo. RG41 48 A3
Doles Hill. RG41 48 A6
Doles La. RG41 48 A5
Dorset Way. RG41 48 A3
Duncan Dri. RG40 49 G4
Dunkirk Clo. RG41 48 A3
Durham Clo. RG41 48 A3
Dyer Rd. RG40 49 G2
Eagle Clo. RG41 48 B4
Easthampstead Rd.
 RG40 49 F3
Eastheath Av. RG40 48 D5
Eastheath Gdns. RG41 48 D5
Elizabeth Rd. RG40 49 F3
Ellison Way. RG40 49 E3
Elms Rd. RG40 49 E4
Emerald Clo. RG41 48 A2
Emm Clo. RG41 48 B1
Emmbrook Gate. RG41 48 C1
Emmbrook Rd. RG41 48 C1
Emmview Clo. RG41 48 C2
Erica Dri. RG40 49 F4
Essame Clo. RG40 49 F3
Eustace Cres. RG40 49 F1
Evendons Clo. RG41 48 D6
Evendons La. RG41 48 C6
Evergreen Way. RG41 48 C4
Fairview Rd. RG40 49 E4
Falcon Way. RG41 48 B3
Finchampstead Rd.
 RG40 48 D6
Fishponds Clo. RG41 48 C5
Fishponds Rd. RG41 48 C5
Flamingo Clo. RG41 48 B4
Fleet Clo. RG41 48 B3
Foxglove Clo. RG41 48 A2
Frederick Pl. RG41 48 D3
Freesia Clo. RG41 48 A2
Froghall Dri. RG40 49 G3
Gadd Clo. RG40 49 G2
Gipsy La. RG40 49 E4
Glebelands Rd. RG40 49 E2
Glendale Clo. RG41 48 D6
Goodchild Rd. RG40 49 F3
Goodrings Grn. RG40 49 H3
Gorrick Sq. RG41 48 D6
Green Croft. RG40 49 G1
Green Dri. RG40 49 G4
Gull Clo. RG41 48 B4
Hampshire Way. RG41 48 A3
Harmar Clo. RG40 49 G3
Hart Dyke Clo. RG41 48 D6
Havelock Rd. RG41 48 B3
Hawkes Clo. RG41 48 C2
Hawkins Way. RG41 48 C2
Hazel Clo. RG41 48 B4
Heath Rd. RG41 48 D2
Heathlands Rd. RG40 49 G6
Heddington Clo. RG40 49 F1
Heddington Dri. RG41 49 F1
Heelas Rd. RG41 48 C3
Heron Rd. RG41 48 B3
Herons Way. RG40 49 G2
Hertford Clo. RG41 48 A4
Highfield Clo. RG40 49 E3
Holly Orchard. RG41 48 C4
Holmes Clo. RG41 48 C5
Holmes Cres. RG41 48 C5
Holt La. RG41 48 D2
Howard Rd. RG40 49 E4
Hughes Rd. RG40 49 G2
Humber Clo. RG41 48 B2
Huntingdonshire Clo.
 RG41 48 A3
Hutsons Clo. RG40 49 F1

INDUSTRIAL & RETAIL:
 Mulberry Business Park.
  RG41 48 C
 Oaklands Park Ind Est.
  RG41 48 C
 Station Ind Est. RG40 48 D
 The Business Centre.
  RG41 48 D
Japonica Clo. RG41 48 A
Jasmine Clo. RG40 48 D
Jubilee Av. RG40 48 D
Jupiter Way. RG41 48 B
Jutland Clo. RG41 48 B
Keephatch Rd. RG40 49 G
Kendrick Clo. RG40 49 E
Kennet Ct. RG41 48 B
Kent Clo. RG41 48 A
Kesteven Way. RG41 48 A
Kestrel Way. RG41 48 B
Lalande Clo. RG41 48 B
Landen Ct. RG41 48 C
Langborough Rd. RG40 49 E
Larch Av. RG41 48 C
Larkspur Clo. RG41 48 A
Latimer Rd. RG41 48 C
Laud Way. RG40 49 G
Laurel Clo. RG41 48 B
Lawrence Clo. RG40 49 F
Lenny Clo. RG41 49 F
Lime Clo. RG41 48 C
Limmerhill Rd. RG41 48 B
Linden Clo. RG40 48 E
Lindsey Clo. RG41 48 A
Linnet Walk. RG41 48 B
London Rd. RG40 49 F
Longs Way. RG40 49 C
Lowther Clo. RG41 48 E
Lowther Rd. RG41 48 E
Luckley Path. RG40 49 E
Luckley Rd. RG41 48 D
Luckley Wood. RG41 49 C
Macphail Dri. RG40 49 C
Magnolia Way. RG41 48 B
Mansfield Rd. RG41 48 C
Market Pl. RG40 49 E
Marks Rd. RG41 48 C
Mars Clo. RG41 48 B
Martins Dri. RG41 48 D

Matthewsgreen Rd.
 RG41 48
Mays Rd. RG40 49
Meadow Rd. RG41 48
Meadow Walk. RG41 48
Meadow Way. RG41 48
Medina Clo. RG41 48
Medway Clo. RG41 48
Mercury Av. RG41 48
Mill Clo. RG41 48
Millmead. RG41 48
Milton Dri. RG40 48
Milton Gdns. RG40 48
Milton Rd. RG40 48
Minden Clo. RG40 48
Moles Clo. RG40 49
Molly Millars Bri. RG41 48
Molly Millars Clo. RG41 48
Molly Millars La. RG41 48
Monkshood Clo. RG40 49
Mons Clo. RG41 49
Montague Clo. RG40 49
Moores Grn. RG40 49
Mount Pleasant. RG41 48
Mower Clo. RG40 49
Murdoch Rd. RG40 49
Murray Rd. RG41 49
Mylne Sq. RG40 49
Neptune Clo. RG41 48
Norfolk Clo. RG41 48
Norreys Av. RG40 49
North Way. RG41 48
Norton Rd. RG40 49
Oakey Dri. RG40 49
Oaklands Dri. RG41 48
Oaklands Park. RG41 48
Old Forest Rd. RG41 48
Old Woosehill La. RG41 48
Opal Way. RG41 48
Orchard Clo. RG40 49
Orchard Pl. RG40 49
Ormonde Rd. RG40 49
Osborne Rd. RG40 49
Osterley Clo. RG40 49
Owl Clo. RG41 49
Oxford Rd. RG40 49

ages Croft. RG40	49 F4		Richmond Rise. RG41	48 A2		Smiths Walk. RG41	48 B3
aice Grn. RG40	49 F2		Riding Way. RG41	48 A3		Snowberry Clo. RG41	48 C4
almer School Rd.			Roberts Gro. RG41	48 C5		Somerset Clo. RG41	48 A3
RG40	49 E3		Rook Clo. RG41	48 B4		Sorrell Clo. RG40	49 G1
ark Av. RG40	48 D3		Rose St. RG40	49 E3		South Clo. RG40	49 F4
ark Rd. RG40	48 D3		Rosebay. RG40	49 G1		South Dri. RG40	49 F4
atten Ash Dri. RG40	49 G2		Rotherfield Av. RG41	48 C2		Southlands Clo. RG40	49 F4
ayley Dri. RG40	49 G1		Roundabout La. RG41	48 A1		Southlands Rd. RG40	49 F4
each St. RG40	49 E3		Rowan Clo. RG41	48 B4		Southwood. RG40	49 F5
eregrine Clo. RG41	48 B4		Ruby Clo. RG41	48 A2		Sparrow Clo. RG41	48 B4
erkins Way. RG41	48 C4		Ruskin Way. RG41	48 A3		Spencer Clo. RG41	48 A3
etrel Clo. RG41	48 B4		Sadlers La. RG41	48 A1		Stanley Rd. RG40	49 G3
hoenix Clo. RG41	48 B3		St Heliers Clo. RG41	48 D6		Starling Clo. RG41	48 B4
gott Rd. RG40	49 F1		St Pauls Gate. RG41	48 C3		Starmead Dri. RG40	49 F4
ough La. RG40	49 H2		Sandy La. RG41	48 A5		Station Rd. RG40	48 D3
over Clo. RG41	48 B4		Sapphire Clo. RG41	48 A2		Staverton Clo. RG40	49 H3
oppy Pl. RG40	49 E3		Sarum Cres. RG40	49 F2		Stephanie Chase Ct.	
urslane. RG40	49 H3		Saturn Clo. RG41	48 B3		RG40	49 F2
rke Clo. RG40	49 F3		School Rd. RG41	49 F3		Sturges Rd. RG40	49 F4
uartz Clo. RG41	48 A2		Scots Dri. RG41	48 A1		Suffolk Clo. RG41	48 A3
ances La. RG40	49 G3		Seaford Rd. RG40	49 F3		Sundew Clo. RG40	49 G2
eading Rd. RG41	48 A1		Sewell Av. RG41	48 C1		Swallow Way. RG41	48 B4
ectory Clo. RG40	49 E3		Shefford Cres. RG40	49 F1		Swift Clo. RG41	48 B4
ectory Rd. RG40	49 E3		Sheridan Way. RG41	48 A4		Tamar Way. RG41	48 B3
eeves Way. RG41	48 C5		Shute End. RG40	48 D3		Tamarisk Rise. RG40	49 E2
			Simons La. RG41	48 A2		Tangley Dri. RG41	48 D5
			Sirius Clo. RG41	48 B3		Tanhouse La. RG41	48 C4

Tattersall Clo. RG40	49 G4		Waterloo Rd. RG40	49 G4
The Green. RG41	48 A2		Weavers Ct. RG40	49 E3
The Junipers. RG41	48 A5		Webb Ct. RG40	49 G1
The Rise. RG41	48 C2		Wellington Rd. RG40	48 D3
The Shires. RG41	48 A5		Wescott Rd. RG40	49 F3
The Terrace. RG40	48 D3		Westmorland Clo. RG41	48 A3
Thorpe Clo. RG41	48 D6		Westward Rd. RG41	48 B2
Tigerseye Clo. RG41	48 A2		Whaley Rd. RG40	49 G1
Topaz Clo. RG41	48 A2		Whitebeam Clo. RG41	48 A6
Trafalgar Clo. RG41	48 A3		Willowherb Clo. RG40	49 G2
Trefoil Clo.RG40	49 G2		Wiltshire Dri. RG40	49 F2
Trent Clo. RG41	48 B2		Wiltshire Rd. RG40	49 E1
Trinity Ct. RG41	48 B3		Windmill Av. RG41	48 A1
Tudor Clo. RG40	49 H4		Windmill Clo. RG40	48 B1
Twycross Rd. RG40	49 G2		Winkfield Clo. RG41	48 D6
Twyford Rd. RG40	48 D1		Wisteria Clo. RG41	48 C4
Valley Cres. RG41	48 C1		Woodlands Av. RG41	48 A1
Venus Clo. RG41	48 B3		Woodlands. RG41	48 A5
Villiers Mead. RG41	48 C3		Woodpecker Walk.	
Wallner Way. RG40	49 G4		RG41	48 B4
Walnut Clo. RG41	48 B4		Woodrows Dri. RG40	49 G3
Walnut Ct. RG40	49 E3		Woolf Dri. RG40	49 E2
Walter Rd. RG41	48 A1		Woosehill. RG41	48 A3
Ward Clo. RG40	49 F1		Woosehill La. RG41	48 C3
Warren House Rd. RG40	49 F1		Wren Clo. RG41	48 B4
Waterford Way. RG40	49 E3		Yew Clo. RG41	48 B4
Waterloo Cres. RG40	49 G4		Zinnia Clo. RG41	48 A2

ESTATE PUBLICATIONS

RED BOOKS

ALDERSHOT, CAMBERLEY
ALFRETON, BELPER, RIPLEY
ASHFORD, TENTERDEN
BANGOR, CAERNARFON
BARNSTAPLE, ILFRACOMBE
BASILDON, BILLERICAY
BASINGSTOKE, ANDOVER
BATH, BRADFORD-ON-AVON
BEDFORD
BIRMINGHAM, WOLVERHAMPTON, COVENTRY
BOURNEMOUTH, POOLE, CHRISTCHURCH
BRACKNELL
BRENTWOOD
BRIGHTON, LEWES, NEWHAVEN, SEAFORD
BRISTOL
BROMLEY (London Bromley)
BURTON-UPON-TRENT, SWADLINCOTE
BURY ST. EDMUNDS
CAMBRIDGE
CARDIFF
CARLISLE
CHELMSFORD, BRAINTREE, MALDON, WITHAM
CHESTER
CHESTERFIELD
CHICHESTER, BOGNOR REGIS
COLCHESTER, CLACTON
CORBY, KETTERING
CRAWLEY & MID SUSSEX
CREWE
DERBY, HEANOR, CASTLE DONINGTON
EASTBOURNE, BEXHILL, SEAFORD, NEWHAVEN
EDINBURGH, MUSSELBURGH, PENICUIK
EXETER, EXMOUTH
FALKIRK, GRANGEMOUTH
FAREHAM, GOSPORT
FLINTSHIRE TOWNS
FOLKESTONE, DOVER, DEAL & ROMNEY MARSH
GLASGOW, & PAISLEY
GLOUCESTER, CHELTENHAM
GRAVESEND, DARTFORD
GRAYS, THURROCK
GREAT YARMOUTH, LOWESTOFT
GRIMSBY, CLEETHORPES
GUILDFORD, WOKING
HARLOW, BISHOPS STORTFORD
HASTINGS, BEXHILL, RYE
HEREFORD
HERTFORD, HODDESDON, WARE
HIGH WYCOMBE
HUNTINGDON, ST. NEOTS
IPSWICH, FELIXSTOWE
ISLE OF MAN
ISLE OF WIGHT TOWNS
KENDAL
KIDDERMINSTER
KINGSTON-UPON-HULL
LANCASTER, MORECAMBE
LEICESTER, LOUGHBOROUGH
LINCOLN
LLANDUDNO, COLWYN BAY
LUTON, DUNSTABLE
MACCLESFIELD
MAIDSTONE
MANSFIELD, MANSFIELD WOODHOUSE
MEDWAY, GILLINGHAM
MILTON KEYNES
NEW FOREST TOWNS
NEWPORT, CHEPSTOW
NEWTOWN, WELSHPOOL
NORTHAMPTON
NORTHWICH, WINSFORD
NORWICH
NOTTINGHAM, EASTWOOD, HUCKNALL, ILKESTON
OXFORD, ABINGDON
PENZANCE, ST. IVES
PETERBOROUGH
PLYMOUTH, IVYBRIDGE, SALTASH, TORPOINT
PORTSMOUTH, HAVANT, WATERLOOVILLE
READING
REDDITCH, BROMSGROVE
REIGATE, BANSTEAD, LEATHERHEAD, DORKING

RHYL, PRESTATYN
RUGBY
ST. ALBANS, WELWYN, HATFIELD
SALISBURY, AMESBURY, WILTON
SCUNTHORPE
SEVENOAKS
SHREWSBURY
SITTINGBOURNE, FAVERSHAM, ISLE OF SHEPPEY
SLOUGH, MAIDENHEAD, WINDSOR
SOUTHAMPTON, EASTLEIGH
SOUTHEND-ON-SEA
STAFFORD
STEVENAGE, HITCHIN, LETCHWORTH
STIRLING
STOKE-ON-TRENT
STROUD, NAILSWORTH
SWANSEA, NEATH, PORT TALBOT
SWINDON, CHIPPENHAM, MARLBOROUGH
TAUNTON, BRIDGWATER
TELFORD
THANET, CANTERBURY, HERNE BAY, WHITSTABLE
TORBAY (Torquay, Paignton, Newton Abbot)
TRURO, FALMOUTH
TUNBRIDGE WELLS, TONBRIDGE, CROWBOROUGH
WARWICK, ROYAL LEAMINGTON SPA &
   STRATFORD UPON AVON
WATFORD, HEMEL HEMPSTEAD
WELLINGBOROUGH
WESTON-SUPER-MARE, CLEVEDON
WEYMOUTH, DORCHESTER
WINCHESTER, NEW ARLESFORD
WORCESTER, DROITWICH
WORTHING, LITTLEHAMPTON, ARUNDEL
WREXHAM
YORK

COUNTY RED BOOKS (Town Centre Maps)

BEDFORDSHIRE
BERKSHIRE
BUCKINGHAMSHIRE
CAMBRIDGESHIRE
CHESHIRE
CORNWALL
DERBYSHIRE
DEVON
DORSET
ESSEX
GLOUCESTERSHIRE
HAMPSHIRE
HEREFORDSHIRE
HERTFORDSHIRE
KENT
LEICESTERSHIRE & RUTLAND
LINCOLNSHIRE
NORFOLK
NORTHAMPTONSHIRE
NOTTINGHAMSHIRE
OXFORDSHIRE
SHROPSHIRE
SOMERSET
STAFFORDSHIRE
SUFFOLK
SURREY
SUSSEX (EAST)
SUSSEX (WEST)
WILTSHIRE
WORCESTERSHIRE

OTHER MAPS

KENT TO CORNWALL (1:460,000)
CHINA (1:6,000,000)
INDIA (1:3,750,000)
INDONESIA (1:4,000,000)
NEPAL (1,800,000)
SOUTH EAST ASIA (1:6,000,000)
THAILAND (1:1,600,000)

STREET PLANS

EDINBURGH TOURIST PLAN
ST. ALBANS

OFFICIAL TOURIST & LEISURE MAPS

SOUTH EAST ENGLAND (1:200,000)
KENT & EAST SUSSEX (1:150,000)
SUSSEX & SURREY (1:150,000)
SUSSEX (1:50,000)
SOUTHERN ENGLAND (1:200,000)
ISLE OF WIGHT (1:50,000)
WESSEX (1:200,000)
DORSET (1:50,000)
DEVON & CORNWALL (1:200,000)
CORNWALL (1:180,000)
DEVON (1:200,000)
DARTMOOR & SOUTH DEVON COAST (1:100,000)
EXMOOR & NORTH DEVON COAST (1:100,000)
GREATER LONDON M25 (1:80,000)
EAST ANGLIA (1:200,000)
CHILTERNS & THAMES VALLEY (1:200,000)
THE COTSWOLDS (1:110,000)
COTSWOLDS & SEVERN VALLEY (1:200,000)
WALES (1:250,000)
CYMRU (1:250,000)
THE SHIRES OF MIDDLE ENGLAND (1:250,000)
THE MID SHIRES (Staffs, Shrops, etc.) (1:200,000)
PEAK DISTRICT (1:100,000)
SNOWDONIA (1:125,000)
YORKSHIRE (1:200,000)
YORKSHIRE DALES (1:125,000)
NORTH YORKSHIRE MOORS (1:125,000)
NORTH WEST ENGLAND (1:200,000)
ISLE OF MAN (1:60,000)
NORTH PENNINES & LAKES (1:200,000)
LAKE DISTRICT (1:75,000)
BORDERS OF ENGLAND & SCOTLAND (1:200,000)
BURNS COUNTRY (1:200,000)
HEART OF SCOTLAND (1:200,000)
GREATER GLASGOW (1:150,000)
EDINBURGH & THE LOTHIANS (1:150,000)
ISLE OF ARRAN (1:63,360)
FIFE (1:100,000)
LOCH LOMOND & TROSSACHS (1:150,000)
ARGYLL THE ISLES & LOCH LOMOND (1:275,000)
PERTHSHIRE, DUNDEE & ANGUS (1:150,000)
FORT WILLIAM, BEN NEVIS, GLEN COE (1:185,000)
IONA (1:10,000) & MULL (1:115,000)
GRAMPIAN HIGHLANDS (1:185,000)
LOCH NESS & INVERNESS (1:150,000)
AVIEMORE & SPEY VALLEY (1:150,000)
SKYE & LOCHALSH (1:130,000)
ARGYLL & THE ISLES (1:200,000)
CAITHNESS & SUTHERLAND (1:185,000)
HIGHLANDS OF SCOTLAND (1:275,000)
WESTERN ISLES (1:125,000)
ORKNEY & SHETLAND (1:128,000)
ENGLAND & WALES (1:650,000)
SCOTLAND (1:500,000)
HISTORIC SCOTLAND (1:500,000)
SCOTLAND CLAN MAP (1:625,000)
BRITISH ISLES (1:1,100,000)
GREAT BRITAIN (1:1,100,000)

EUROPEAN LEISURE MAPS

EUROPE (1:3,100,000)
BENELUX (1:600,000)
FRANCE (1:1,000,000)
GERMANY (1:1,000,000)
IRELAND (1:625,000)
ITALY (1:1,000,000)
SPAIN & PORTUGAL (1,1,000,000)
CROSS CHANNEL VISITORS' MAP (1:530,000)
WORLD (1:35,000,000)
WORLD FLAT

TOWNS IN NORTHERN FRANCE STREET ATLAS
BOULOGNE SHOPPERS MAP
CALAIS SHOPPERS MAP
DIEPPE SHOPPERS MAP

ESTATE PUBLICATIONS are also
Distributors in the UK for:

INTERNATIONAL TRAVEL MAPS, Canada
HALLWAG, Switzerland
ORDNANCE SURVEY

Catalogue and prices from:
ESTATE PUBLICATIONS
Bridewell House, Tenterden, Kent. TN30 6EP.
Tel: 01580 764225   Fax: 01580 763720
www.estate-publications.co.uk